Are We Having Fun Yet?

Jack
Hope you enjoy the book.
Bonnie Draper

Are We Having Fun Yet?

*A Woman's View Of Life In Canada's Far North,
Where Men Are Men And Women Are Too!*

Bonnie Traplin

Red Anvil Press

Copyright © 2004 Bonnie Traplin
All rights reserved. No part of this publication, except brief excerpts for purpose of review, may be reproduced, stored in a retrieval system, or transmitted in any form or by any means, electronic, mechanical, photocopying, recording, or otherwise, without the prior written permission of the publisher.

RED ANVIL PRESS

1393 Old Homestead Drive, Second Floor
Oakland, Oregon 97462-9506.
E-MAIL: editor@elderberrypress. com
TEL/FAX: 541. 459. 6043
www. elderberrypress. com

Red Anvil books are available from your favorite bookstore, amazon. com, or from our 24 hour order line: 1. 800. 431. 1579

Library of Congress Control Number:
Publisher's Catalog-in-Publication Data
Are We Having Fun Yet?/Bonnie Traplin
ISBN 1932762256
1. Memoir.
2. Yukon.
3. Wilderness.
4. Adventure.
5. Outdoors.
6. Hunting.
7. Trapping.
8. British Columbia.
I. Title
This book was written, printed and bound in the United States of America.

For my loving husband Ted
Thank you for your patience
your wisdom and your strength
For without you I would not be here
I wouldn't have missed it for anything
You are truly my hero

For my mom who thought my letters worth saving
and asked me to put them into book form

For my dad from whom I inherited my itchy feet and my love of
British Columbia

For George our best friend and mentor with whom we shared
our lives for so many years

And in memory of our beloved Goldy
you are dearly loved
you are greatly missed
you will never be forgotten
my dear, dear friend
thank you

Introduction

My husband Ted and I were married in Owen Sound, Ontario in June of 1975. Two months later we had everything we owned packed, and were on our way to British Columbia.

Having spent much of my youth as the daughter of missionarys living in remote areas of Northern British Columbia and at times in Ontario, returning to British Columbia would be a welcome homecoming for me. In the years since I had left this amazingly beautiful country I had never lost my yearning to return to it.

Ted on the other hand, was born and raised in Ontario, and had never been to British Columbia. As an avid outdoorsman, hunter and fisherman, he could hardly wait. Although having been raised in a fairly large town, we had no fear that Ted would have any trouble adjusting to the lifestyle we had chosen for our future.

Our intentions were to head as far North in British Columbia as we could make it before our funds ran out, then, we would settle down and start our new life together. Due to a car accident and the Insurance Company of British Columbia being on strike, Kamloops, a thriving cattle town in British Columbia's interior was as far as we were able to go.

We were devastated with this turn of events and had no choice but to make the best of our situation. Needing work, Ted took many jobs over the next few years to make ends meet. These jobs included working in a sporting goods distributorship, the peat moss bogs of Alberta, the oil rigs in Northern Alberta and a plywood plant in central British Columbia. I took many small Jobs during this time to help meet expenses and to try and save some money. Not once during this time did our dreams of moving north fade.

Now, five and a half years, two provinces, and many small towns later, we were once again ready to head North. This time we had a destination in mind. Atlin, the last utopia, the Switzerland of the north would be our home for the next nine years.

This is the story of two green horns with a dream. The story of a woman's view of survival in the wilderness; from building our first log cabin together and living off of the land, to a winter spent on a trap line in a cabin built in the late 1800's and originally used as a line cabin when the historic telegraph trail was being pushed through this area.

This story tells of big game hunters in remote wilderness camps and pack strings of horses that were often our only means of transportation.

It is the story of how we learned to survive the challenges of every day living in the North and grew to love the simple things in life. How, by experiencing this lifestyle, we developed a special bond of closeness that grew from a total reliance on each other for day to day survival until we became not only husband and wife but each other's constant companion and best friend.

Chapter 1

Our Arrival

It was in April of 1981 when my husband Ted and I finally arrived in the North. We were on our way to fulfilling our longtime dreams.

Once again we had with us almost everything we owned. Besides the few boxes of electrical appliances we had stored with friends in Alberta, our worldly possessions consisted of an old G. M. C. four by four pickup truck with a homemade camper on its back, the campers contents, and a bank account of almost fifteen hundred dollars.

The money seemed like a fortune to us and had taken almost five years to save. We didn't know it then, but the first cabin we would build, would cost us twelve hundred dollars of our hard earned savings for roofing paper, plywood, nails and insulation.

We were all set. We had the camper to live in and planned to hunt and fish for most of our food. We had brought a few staples with us, including twenty five pounds of brown rice, a couple hundred pounds of flour and five pounds of every type of dried bean imaginable. According to the research we had done on wilderness survival, these items were all necessities, and during our years in the North, we ate them often and in many different forms. To this day neither of us care to see beans or brown rice again in any form.

While living in central British Columbia years earlier we had decided to buy a quarter horse. We met George and his wife Goldy when we went to look at a horse they had for sale. The horse was perfect and the meeting resulted in our lifelong friendship with George and Goldy.

Before we left to head North, we had made arrangements to meet our long time friend George Reed at the homestead of his friends Dick and Holly, twenty miles North of Atlin.

Excitement was high as we reached our turn off of the Alaska highway and started to head South down the Atlin road. Although we were still in the Yukon Territory, just sixty miles from Whitehorse, this woud be the final stage of our journey. The winding, narrow, dirt road would meander through the Yukon and back into British Columbia following the shores of both Little and Big Atlin Lakes. At the roads end we would find the historic gold rush town of Atlin, British Columbia.

Dick and Holly's homestead turned out to be hard to find as it was set quite a way back in from the main road, and as luck would have it, we missed it and ended up in the little village of Atlin itself.

Tired as we were from our long journey, our first glimpse of Atlin clinging to the edge of picturesque Atlin Lake made our long trip worthwhile. Snowcapped Atlin Mountain with it's uniquely scarred face stands majestically alone directly across from the little town. Between the town and the mountain are three small islands with their mirror images reflected in the still waters around them.

The town itself takes one back to a time of sleepy log cabins with wood smoke drifting lazily upward from every chimney. The large wood piles in each yard, tell the story of the long, cold winter ahead.

In front of one tiny, weathered log cabin, stands a post with two interesting sets of moose horns on display, still locked in their final battle for supremacy. Not far away, mounted over another doorway, hangs another unique set of moose horns that have wire from the historic telegraph trail wrapped firmly around them, the obvious cause of the animals demise.

Farther along the dusty, pothole covered street, stands a rustic well aged cabin surrounded by a tumbling down, faded, board fence. It's yard was piled high with many bleached moose and caribou horns, with the overflow stacked high on the cabin's roof.

Large Malamute type dogs and shaggy mountain horses well versed in wilderness survival, roamed the town at will, the horses nibbling on the tall clumps of grass and bits of year old gardens. Most of the land in the North is open range land and one must fence in any land one does not want stray horses wandering around on. The locals find the horses are beneficial in the cleaning up of year old gardens and bits of grass that pass for lawns, so they let them roam.

As we paused to take in all of these quaint but typically Northern sights, the sensation of stepping back into time was overwhelming and the feeling of coming home swept over us both.

By this time it was getting fairly late so we turned the truck around and once again tried to find the homestead we had missed. Finally, arriving at its gates around midnight, and after taking one look at the muddy trail passing as the lane leading to the ranch, we knew that this was the end of our trail for the day. Parking the truck, we set up the camper for the night, and crawled thankfully into our sleeping bags.

By dawn we had dug out our ever present rubber gum boots, a necessity in this country, and were slipping and sliding through six inches of mud, down the lane towards the ranch. As we rounded the first bend the tranquillity of the postcard like scene that greeted us left us both breathless. This is what we had come North to find. Before us lay a narrow, winding, dirt trail, leading through a natural, snow covered meadow towards a small honey colored log cabin with wood smoke drifting gently upward from its chimney. The hills behind the cabin were blanketed in first growth timber and all this wondrous beauty was surrounded by majestic, snow capped mountains. Pausing to soak up the beauty of our surroundings, an overwhelming sense of peace filled our souls.

As we neared the magical little cabin the wolf like howling of a dozen sled dogs heralded our arrival. Each of the large furry animals was attached to its own log dog house by a long length of heavy chain. The noise that twelve, howling, excited dogs can make is unbelievable and until one gets accustomed to the dogs they can be quite terrifying as they run around barking, growling, and constantly lunging at the end of their chains. I, for one, was glad the chains were sturdy. Most of the sled dogs in this area are a mixture of Malamute, Husky and Indian village dogs. They range in size from very large to quite small, size does not affect their ability to pull a sled at all.

The fuss that the sled dogs were making had warned everyone inside the cabin that we were on our way. George, Dick and Holly were waiting for us with a toasty fire going and breakfast simmering on the wood cook stove. With the mouthwatering smell of bacon filling every corner of the cabin, we could hardly wait to sit down and eat.

From the first moment we saw it, we were enchanted by the little log cabin. This was the first cabin of its type that either of us had ever seen. We found it to be cozy, warm, and extremely homey. This cabin was our dream home and right away we made plans to build one of our own.

Land in northern British Columbia was open to homesteading if a person followed the governments staking laws. To stake land, one had to measure out the land, mark all of the boundaries, and then figure out how much of the staked land would be classified as arable. We then had to submit a plan to the British Columbia Lands Department down South in Smithers advising them of the location of the land; how much we planned on clearing; to what use we planned on putting the land; what buildings we planned on erecting; and when we planned on having all of the above finished. Next, we had to tell them how long we would take to fence in the entire piece. Finally we had to wait for the land inspector to arrive on his once a year trip to do soil testing. The Fish and Wildlife staff had to do an extensive survey, often using helicopters, to decide if letting us have the land would interfere with the wildlife in the area. Fish and Wildlife also had to approve the type of fences we planned on building to make sure the areas wildlife could jump them without being injured or getting hung up in them. This entire process could be done in a period of two years if one was lucky, but more often than not the final outcome of the whole thing was the government asked you to locate a different piece of land and start all over again.

Chances were that the land we had staked would never support any kind of crop anyway because of the short, dry, growing season of approximately sixty frost free days a year. One person we know plowed and seeded twenty acres in hay. At harvest time he ended up with twelve bales of hay, and that was total, not per acre. So, as you can see, staking land in the North is a long drawn out process and it takes a persistent person to succeed.

During the next few days we set up our camper in a Fireweed covered meadow ringed by tall, first growth Lodge Pole pine trees. This would give us privacy and a place to call home until we could get organized and build our own dream cabin. We had decided to build a cabin on a piece of land belonging to Dick and Holly's homestead, and then when our own land was approved and our cabin built, Dick would buy this one from us and use it for his guests.

During the three months it took to build the cabin, we lived in our camper. Temperatures dropped as low as minus forty degrees Fahrenheit. As we had no furnace or any other means of heat in the camper, we quickly learned to leave the Coleman lantern burning throughout the night. Amazingly enough, most nights the lantern could keep the camper temperature above zero. As the lantern would, without fail, run out of fuel before morning, we would awaken either soaked in condensation or with our sleeping bags frozen to our plywood bunks.

The trail leading past our camper was used nightly as a runway for a fair size pack of timber wolves. One wolf we shot out of this pack was seven feet ten inches long, and he wasn't the largest in this particular pack. The wolf we shot was almost pure white and others in the pack were silver, brown and black.

During this time we helped Dick and Holly haul logs out of the bush with Dick's Yamaha 340 trappers model snowmobile. While the men cut and hauled logs, Holly and I peeled them. Peeling logs consisted of straddling each log while we used a two handled draw knife to peel off all of the bark. This was hard work as we had to turn each log as we went to get the bark off. This process is much the same as peeling a carrot, except that just under the bark of a tree is a layer of sticky pitch that gets on everything it touches, and it's about impossible to remove from one's skin and hair. These logs were to be used in building a huge sixteen foot by thirty six foot greenhouse.

With the greenhouse project finished we all pitched in and helped to build a log ice house. When this was ready, we cut twelve inch by eighteen inch by two foot thick blocks of ice out of Atlin Lake, hauled them the one half mile to the road by snowmobile and sled and then loaded them into the back of our pickup truck. It was amazing how much ice it took to fill the eight foot by twelve foot ice house! In fact the following fall when it was again time to fill the ice house, we discovered the majority of ice was still left inside.

With the ice house finished, Ted, George, and I hopped in George's pickup and headed back down the Alaska highway, arriving in Ponoka, Alberta, on Easter weekend. George's wife, Goldy had a lovely Easter dinner ready for us all. One week later Ted and I returned to Atlin with George's two thousand gallon water truck that Ted had previously driven in the oil fields of northern Alberta. Ted, eventually put it to work during the construction of the new Atlin airport.

Before we left Alberta with the water truck, we enlarged the hole in the tank's top and loaded the tank with groceries, canning jars, sacks of oats and hundred pound sacks of potatoes. George planned to sell the oats and potatoes in Atlin. We then used any spare space we could find to load building supplies that we would need for our cabin, as everything is much more expensive in the North. It took Ted thirty one hours of driving to get us home to Atlin. He did all the driving and took only one four hour stopover to rest. Arriving early in the morning, we could see that the lane was still impassable with mud so we parked at the gate and caught a couple of hours sleep. Feeling better, we dug out our faithful old gum boots and set off down the lane. Upon our arrival at Dick and Holly's cabin, we discovered that only Holly was home. Dick was at a friends thirty five miles away gelding a horse for them.

Holly hooked up the sled dogs to their sleds and helped us pull all the supplies up the long lane to the cabin where we could unload them and keep them from freezing. It was quite the sight watching the dogs pull the loaded sleds through all the mud.

Chapter 2

Building Our Cabin

The first days of our return from Alberta were spent clearing trees, burning brush, and trying to level off the ground as much as possible at our chosen cabin site. The spot we selected was ringed by a crescent of tall, first growth, Lodge Pole Pine trees. It faced cleared fields, natural meadows, and the rugged snowcapped Black, Minto, and Hitchcock mountains. Ted and I would enjoy many hunting, fishing, and backpacking trips on these mountains in the future. Ted would eventually shoot his first sheep on one of them, supplementing our diet with the meat. Sheep meat is the best of all wild meat and was always a welcome treat.

```
Dear Mom and Dad,
May 19, 1981
```

We have been keeping busy as we've started to build our cabin. What a job! Peeling all the logs has to be the hardest thing I've ever done in my life! I don't have one little spot on my entire body that's not either bruised, scraped, sore or covered in sticky pitch. This cabin won't be large, but will do until we can get some staked land approved for our own use by the government and can build on it. When we're finished, we will have two rooms downstairs and a loft above the kitchen for sleeping. The cabin should be cute, cozy and quite comfortable. We don't have any furniture but I don't think it'll matter much as we are outside most of the time anyway.

As I look back, I can't help but think about how our outlook toward what was a necessity, and what wasn't, had changed to suit our environment in a short time.

During this time of hard work, we took enough time off to go fishing and hunt rabbits for food. We usually fished in the two small lakes located not too far behind our homestead.

We went fishing the other evening on a picturesque little lake within a fifteen minute hike of our camper. The crystal clear mirror-like images in the still water reflected the rock bluff around the lake. Rolling hills and densely timbered slopes surrounded it. Ted caught two nice Northern Pike. One was about five pounds and the other around four. They were sure good eating! This is high praise indeed coming from two people who aren't particularly fond of any fish.

We took a couple of Dick and Holly's sled dogs fishing with us. They really are smart! Both dogs swam across the lake four different times as they followed our canoe. This is a distance of about one quarter mile for each crossing. The largest dog, Taku, a long-haired Malamute, caught his own fish, and if I hadn't watched him catch it, I wouldn't have believed it possible. What he did was play with the three or four pound fish until it was close enough to shore for him to pick it up in his mouth. Then he swam all the way back across the lake with it wiggling in his mouth. When he was far enough away from Scout, the other dog who was trying to get the fish away from him, he set the fish down and proceeded to eat it.

The next night Ted walked back to the same lake again, but as I was tired I stayed at the camper. This time he caught two more nice fish and while relaxing watched a moose feeding on weeds at the water's edge. This was an unforgettable experience as there is no moose in the area of Ontario that we came from.

Fishing was a necessity to supplement our diet and dwindling food supplies, so it was very serious business. Since hunting season wasn't going to open until August, our diet at the moment consisted mainly of rabbit, Snowshoe Hare, fish such as Northern Pike and Lake trout, and two kinds of grouse, Ruffed and Franklin.

These supplemented the brown rice and beans that we had brought back with us from Alberta. There were also lots of ducks and geese around at this time of the year, but because they were nesting we didn't hunt them.

```
Atlin Lake is still frozen over and we are anx-
iously awaiting breakup. The Loons have returned
to the smaller lakes now so spring is finally on
the way. We love, listening to the hauntingly lonely
sounds of the Loons calling to each other. Ted is
getting quite good at imitating them and can even
get them to answer him.
```

We did a lot of exploring during these first days of spring and found the remains of several log cabins and root cellars.

We picked up lots of old bottles and insulators along the historic telegraph trail, hauled all of our treasures home, cleaned them, and put them to good use in the kitchen. We visited the Atlin Museum and discovered many labor saving devices that the old-timers had used, which would have simplified our lives tremendously if they were still available for use. One of my favorites was a hand-cranked washing machine that could have saved many hours of hard work on wash day. We enjoyed those times of relaxation shared together, but spent most of our time working on our cabin. We worked through the end of May and into June. After the trees had been cut down and the limbs cut off, they were pulled out of the bush using a strong cable hooked onto the back of our pickup truck. Then they all had to be peeled. Since by now I had lots of practice peeling logs, this turned out to be my job. The next step was to lay out the floor. We did this by notching logs together to make a level base over which we laid insulation and then the plywood floor.

The notching and levelling of the floor turned into quite the chore and took lots of skill with a chain saw. With this done, it was time to start the log work on the walls. The log work turned out to be unbelievably hard work, harder on Ted then on me by far, as he had to do most of the heavy work. We had chosen to build this cabin with Hudson Bay corners. Hudson Bay corners consist of two 2x10s fastened together at right angles in each corner. Spikes are driven through these boards and into the end of each log to hold them in place. The logs are also spiked vertically to each other. When the cabin was finished, logs were squared off to fit into these corners to conceal the boards. My main job at this point, consisted of helping Ted lift each heavy, green log into place, and then hold it steady when Ted climbed up on top of it and hammered in the required number of spikes.

This process sounds much easier than it is in reality. Many times, by the end of the day, tempers were short, and tears were plentiful. The higher the log walls got, the harder it was to hold the logs so they didn't roll off while Ted climbed up on them. Keep in mind, green logs are extremely heavy. After this, the insulation was cut into strips the same width as the logs, and was laid on top of each one and stuffed into any cracks or openings, to block out drafts and to help the cabin stay warm. As the logs aged and settled into place they would shrink and the installation process would have to be repeated many times over the next few years. During this time of hard work, water had to be hauled from the river a good half-mile away in a five-gallon metal bucket and then heated on a wood fire. Our evening sponge baths in the dishpan turned out to be lots of work but were always appreciated. As tired as we were from all of our cabin building, bathing was the highlight of our day during the installation process, for fiberglass insulation has a way of getting into every pore and seems to fill eyes, ears, and even one's mouth. A lot of our conversations at this point centered around the joys of hot and cold running water and a real bath tub.

```
June 6, 1981
Dear mom and dad,
```
We have been working extremely hard and are almost ready to start putting the roof on the cabin. I can't believe Ted and I have actually accomplished what we have. We have both learned one thing from this experience and that is that building a cabin, even a small one, is no small undertaking. It takes a lot of good hard work and determination.

Many times I've felt like just sitting down and giving up. We spent last week cutting boards for the roof and the kitchen cupboards. What miserable back breaking work! Many times I would just sit and cry. Often I wished I was anywhere else but here.

At this point the one question that keeps flickering through my mind is, are we having fun yet? The first thing we did was locate some big Spruce trees and cut down the biggest one we could find. Some of the trees we fell were 100 feet tall and 10 feet around. This was quite a challenge for two beginners. Once down, the easy part was finished as we then had to saw them into 11 foot lengths and remove the limbs from all of them. All of the limbs had to be pulled away from the working area and piled for burning later. We were fortunate to be able to borrow a good chain saw and a portable Alaska saw mill that consisted of a guide that attached to the chain saw bar.

It works this way. First we nailed a 2x8 foot board on top of the eleven foot long log and put shims in it to make it steady. This would be the guide we would use for the initial cut. Next we would set the guide on the saw to the desired thickness of board needed and both of us would push the chain saw and attached guide through the eleven feet of log. This process, was repeated for every board needed. I'm sure my body will never be the same again. I can't imagine how poor Ted feels. Spruce trees in this country grow in bogs and where we were working there were so many black flies and mosquitoes around us that the air was literally black with them. They kept flying in our noses and eyes until we got to the point where we just wanted to scream. I don't know where Ted gets his strength. His endurance never fails to amaze me. I often wonder why we're punishing ourselves.

I know that without Ted doing so much of the heavy work I couldn't go on, I just don't have the physical strength to be more help. After the board cutting process we cut a large log for the centre beam in the roof. This log was about 20 inches in diameter and 32 feet in length. After the large tree had been cut down and limbed, we hooked it to the back of our truck and pulled it out of the bush, back to the cabin and peeled it. Ted then rigged up a pulley system out of rope, and with the help of two friends, we raised the heavy, green log into position and secured it.

I'll send you some pictures when we get the roof on the cabin and you'll be surprised at just how smart we really are. I'm not too sure if you call us smart or just bears for punishment. We think that the cabin is something to be proud of, especially as it's the first thing that either one of us has ever built, city people that we are. Early tomorrow morning, if we can get out of bed, we plan on going bear hunting. We could really use the meat. It would be a nice change from fish and rabbit. I must close for now but I will write more when I can.

Leaving early the next morning, Dick, Holly, Ted, and I set out along a narrow, winding, dirt trail in our pick up. Seven or eight miles up the trail, we arrived at a bridge that consisted of two, 6 inch by 12 foot wooden planks spanning the swollen Fourth of July Creek. Holly and I got out of the truck and stood holding our breath while Ted and Dick lined the truck's tires up on the planks and slowly crept across. Once safely on the other side, we discovered a small, overgrown, wildflower filled meadow. In the meadow stood a rotting log cabin with a dirt floor. Sometime in the distant past, someone had added a weathered board shelf and attached it to the trees just outside of the cabin doorway. Through the gaping hole where a door once hung, one could smell the odor of rotting vegetation and damp earth, along with the various odors of the animals that had wintered inside in past years. Following a narrow, winding valley, we stopped often to glass the miles of rolling, green hillsides with our binoculars. We saw lots of sheep higher on the side hills but, as the season wasn't open for hunting sheep yet, we continued on looking for a bear. A few miles farther on, we decided to split up with Ted and I climbing part way up the hills on one side of the valley and Dick and Holly climbing the other side. Plans were that when we thought we were high enough to have a good view of our surroundings we would find a comfortable spot and sit and glass the hillsides with our binoculars. Ted and I spotted a black bear about the same time that Dick and Holly did and, as the bear was close to where they were sitting, it wasn't long until we heard a shot and saw the bear rolling down the hill. We then watched from our great vantage point as

Holly helped Dick lift the bear onto his back and they set off down the hill toward the pickup truck.

Once home, we skinned the bear and Dick showed Ted how to tan the hide. In order to preserve the meat without refrigeration, we built a smokehouse and used alder twigs to smoke it. It's amazing how long smoked meat will keep and just how delicious it tastes. We rendered the bear fat down to use for lard. The lard rivals the finest supermarket lard in texture, color, and flavor.

```
Ted has been lucky and has been able to find a
couple of weeks work cooking for a gold mine about
ten miles east of Atlin. He learned to cook in a
hurry once they hired him. Must be doing all right
though as he isn't getting any complaints. He comes
home at night and tells me what he has to cook with
the next day and I give him ideas on what he can
make with it.
    The mine employs ten men and is a placer opera-
tion that is removing the overburden prior to set-
ting up their sluice box. He leaves around two
thirty in the morning and doesn't arrive home again
until four in the afternoon, then he puts a couple
of hours work in on the cabin, eats his supper and
hits the bed around seven so he can get up and
ready to leave again at two thirty.
```

Bonnie Traplin

Chapter 3

A Time For Relaxation

While Ted worked at the mine, I rested my weary bones and took advantage of the unusually warm weather.

June 10, 1981
Yesterday Holly and I took two of her horses for a walk and were gone for several hours. As a total greenhorn, I must say it was quite an experience.

This was the first of many exciting times I would have involving horses during our years in the North. Little did I know at this point that in the near future I would be putting roughly fifteen hundred miles a year on a horse in the mountains.

We walked the horses along the edge of Indian River for a while and then swam the river on their backs, followed the shore of Altin lake and meandered along a bush trail home. Trying to stay on the horse's back while it swam the river was sure a funny feeling.
Today Holly and I backpacked into one of the small lakes behind the homestead to go fishing. We were lucky and caught five nice fish. While Holly cleaned the fish we were having for our supper, I

took on the job of sowing the oats and barley by hand in one of the fields. When I say by hand I mean just that. I would reach into the sack and scatter the seeds around myself as I walked. I had a good chuckle as I was doing this as I couldn't help but think how silly I would look to a prairie farmer with all of his huge modern machinery. We'll both finish the sowing tomorrow as the fish are ready to eat now and I'm awfully hungry.

The wild Strawberries and Saskatoon berries are flowering now so it won't be long until we'll have fresh berries to eat. As we don't have a lot of sugar in our diet they will be a real treat. I don't go too far without a gun now that the bears are out of hibernation.

One of the sled dogs was playing with a porcupine the other day. It's always such a fun job pulling all of the quills out. There are porkies all over this area, they are inquisitive, shy, fascinating creatures. The old timers say that porkies are quite tasty but we haven't been that hungry yet. Just kidding! Actually we eat well, but a lot different than we used to. Sometimes I'd give my right arm for a Big Mac and fries and both arms for a diet Coke.

It's light out all of the time right now. As we're not used to it we find it hard to sleep. It's so beautiful here that one hates to waste one's time sleeping anyway. We are only ten days away from the longest day of the year and our sixth anniversary. We hope to get into our cabin before too much longer.

Recently we were fortunate enough to buy some antique windows out of a log building in a ghost town near us. We paid twenty dollars for a whole pile of them. Glass is pretty hard to come by here and the windows we purchased are single pane, hand blown glass. They are full of bubbles and waves that give them a lot of character. Our prize is quite unique and is nine feet wide and seven feet high. It consists of lots of small panes of glass all put together. We'll be using it in the front of the cabin in the twelve foot wall.

I must close for now but will try to get this in the mail the first chance that I get.

June 29, 1981

It's been a while since I've written to you but we've been especially busy getting the cabin to the point where we could finally move into it. It's cute, cozy, and both of us have a feeling of satisfaction with a job well done. The cabin is not big but is comfortable for the two of us, especially after living in the camper for so long. We have two rooms downstairs divided by a log breakfast nook and a loft above the kitchen for sleeping. The living room has an open beam fourteen foot high ceiling that really looks pretty. The cabin's overall size is fourteen feet wide by twenty four feet long, giving us a total of three hundred and thirty six square feet of living space. After living in the camper for so long, it seems huge to us. The big window I told you about in my last letter keeps the cabin nice and bright and gives it a roomy feeling much like bringing the outdoors inside with the cabin's front being almost entirely glass. We don't need the coal oil lamp on anymore. It's amazing just how light it stays. We are enjoying having four walls and a roof again. We still don't have any furniture but we don't miss it at all.

Chapter 4

The Boat

Once we settled into the cabin we found we had a lot more time to investigate our surroundings. Together we took many walks and enjoyed the abundance of wildlife and wildflowers. We took a great many rolls of film.

One day we cut a trail through the bush, hooked an old beat up plywood boat to the back of our pick up, and pulled it into one of the small lakes behind the homestead where we spent a lot of time fishing.

Someone in town was trying to get rid of the boat so they didn't have to haul it to the dump to burn it. They let us have it for twenty five dollars. The price should tell you what kind of shape the boat was in. Getting the boat over the bush trail turned into quite the adventure.

The boat was twenty feet long and sported a plywood cabin with Plexiglas windows perched on top. The trail we cut through the bush ended up having side hills so steep that in some places Ted had to hang off the side of the boat so his weight would keep the boat from tipping over and sliding off of the trailer into the bushes.

Upon our arrival at the lake, we launched our prize, jumped in and away we went, paddling like mad, towards the tiny island at the far end of the lake, with our one and only canoe paddle.

This picturesque little island was the perfect camping spot. Rocky and well treed with a small grassy, wildflower covered meadow amid the trees. The meadow turned out to be the perfect place to pitch our tent. One end of the one acre island was covered in large flat rocks that made a great place for our fire pit and camp kitchen. The large flat rocks surrounding the island were ideal for fishing from or for just stretching out and relaxing on while we lazily watched the fish swim by. Many unforgettable shore lunches of sizzling hot, freshly caught pike were eaten at this spot. We shared a lot of good times here with many of our friends over the years.

The boat turned out to be great fun and stayed afloat as long as one person bailed while the other paddled. We got many hours of enjoyment out of it. Once, while paddling across the lake, our only paddle snapped in half and the paddle end was lost. I quickly grabbed the huge restaurant sized cast iron fry pan that a friend had given us as a gift, and using it as a paddle headed for shore while the others kept on fishing like it was the most natural thing in the world to do.

Every time we arrived at the lake the boat would be sitting on the bottom and had to be bailed out and set afloat before we could use it. We would all hold our breath while Goldy climbed on board, as more often than not, someone would start her laughing at a critical moment and she would end up half submerged in the water as the boat slowly drifted away from the shore.

The hours we spent bailing out the boat were well worth while as we spent many relaxing hours and caught a lot of nice fish out of it. In one day alone we caught roughly sixty pounds of pike. We cooked some for our lunch as there's nothing better than a shore lunch of fresh sizzling hot pike that's been rolled in flour and spices and fried until crisp over an open fire. We always took leftover fish back home with us as we were feeding Holly's fourteen sled dogs while Dick and Holly were in hunting camp. Believe me it takes a lot of fish to feed fourteen hungry dogs.

The dog food was prepared by filling two five gallon metal buckets half full of water from the creek a half mile away. The fish or rabbits were boiled in the buckets over an open fire. During times of plenty, dry dog meal was added to the mixture. Sometimes we fed the dogs the carcasses of porcupines that we had burnt the quills off of or other animals that we acquired from local trappers. Not much goes to waste in this country.

Gradually, the trail that we had cut leading to the lake, became overgrown and could not be seen unless one knew of it's whereabouts. One day while hiking it we came across a tiny little furry grouse chick. I picked it up to get a better look at it and take some pictures when all of a sudden it took off and flew straight to its mom. I was totally amazed that something that small could fly. Another time we came across a bird's nest made out of moose hair that had five baby birds in it. As time went by the trail became an interesting nature walk. Dozens of types of wildflowers grew in abundance and often we would follow fresh bear or moose tracks as we hiked the trail. One day we saw a martin scurrying along a fallen log on the trails edge.

As July turned into August, Ted was able to get a little work helping to build the new Atlin airport. We were always thankful for any work he could get.

Chapter 5

Investigating Our Surroundings

August 21, 1981
Until a couple of weeks ago our weather was a beautiful seventy-five degrees but even then it would cool off pretty good at night, enough that we had to use two or three blankets. Now, it's really getting cold at night and we'll have to do something soon about getting some kind of wood stove to heat the cabin. The wood cook stove that a friend loaned us, keeps us snug and warm in the daytime, but things cool off rapidly when we don't get up to feed it at night.

The airport job didn't last more than a couple of weeks, but again Ted found work in a small sawmill. After he got home from work at night we usually spent a couple of hours getting our winter's wood in. We also took time out daily to either hunt or fish for our next day's food.

We are extremely lucky to have located a nice big patch of Shaggy Mane mushrooms. They are a real treat! In one night alone, Goldy and I cleaned and canned two garbage bags full that the guys had so generously picked and surprised us with. They are so delicious and actually melt in our mouths when rolled in flour and spices and fried until golden and crispy.

By this time George and Goldy had moved to this area and were busy building a two bedroom log house near to our cabin. While Ted and George worked on the house, Goldy and I kept ourselves busy putting food away for the long, cold winter ahead. Both Goldy and George were fountains of information on wilderness survival, having helped settle the remote Anaheim Lake area of central BC many years before.

By now George had acquired a fourteen foot fiberglass boat with a forty horsepower motor, and kept it on Atlin Lake. Ted and I were able to use it whenever we could find the time to do so. The use of the boat made it possible for us to explore the far side of the lake. The lake is about five miles wide at this point and directly across from our cabin was a stretch of the historic mail run trail where not too many years ago, the mail was hauled by dog sled in the winter and by stagecoach the rest of the year. This particular stretch of trail runs from Teslin, Yukon to Whitehorse, Yukon via Atlin, B. C. We always enjoyed investigating this area with its old line cabins and root cellars. Once we were lucky enough to find a perfect mauve glass sealer while investigating the over grown brush area around one old log cabin.

April 21
Well here I am again. I Thought I'd update you as to what's going on in our little corner of the world. Ted and I went backpacking a couple of weeks ago. Our plans were to head up Black and Hitchcock mountains and to do some sheep hunting. The sheep in this area range from Dall to Fannon to Stone and their colors range from pure white to gray to black.
We knew from talking with several of the old-timers in the area, that there were bits and pieces of an old trapper's trail that winds its way part way to our destination. We planned on following this trail as far as we could. After five or six miles of following a long narrow valley between the mountains, we came to a spot where the beavers had flooded the valley making it impossible for us to go any farther. Ted suggested that in order to bypass the beaver flooding we should climb up the

mountain, so, up we went. This strategy worked perfectly until we were a long way above the tree line and I decided to look back to see how high we had climbed. When I took a look and realized where I was I froze solid and could hardly breathe never mind move. I was perched precariously in the center of a huge pile of rocks that had at some time in the past slid part way down the mountain and could start sliding again at any time with the slightest vibration. When Ted finally missed me and realized I was no longer following him and that I was glued to the side of the mountain, he tried coaxing and pleading with me to get me to move, all to no avail for I knew that if I moved the smallest muscle, the whole mountainside would crash down around me. So, I was staying put right where I was. By this time it was getting late in the day and Ted's patience was wearing pretty thin. The straps on the heavy backpack were cutting into my shoulders and the pack itself felt like a lead weight. Finally, fed up and frustrated with me Ted told me to feel free to stay where I was if that was what I'd decided to do and turning he set off down the mountain. Now anger took over for fear, and with tears forgotten and adrenaline pumping it took me all of about two minutes to catch up to him. It's amazing what the thought of being left alone clinging to the side of a mountain all night can do to a person. I kept one step behind him all the way home.

Once back in the safety of our cozy little cabin, we realized that we had taken a wrong turn and that we had completely bypassed the mountain we were looking for, and were on a totally different mountain. So much for our big sheep hunting trip. Both of us were so tired and sore we didn't even leave the cabin for the next couple of days. Ted's shoulders had huge purple bruises on them from the straps of the heavy backpack he was carrying. My shoulders were sore too but the only thing bruised on me was my pride.

Well it's August now and our weather continues

to cool off. The potatoes have frozen in the ground already.

Ted, George and Goldy can now officially be said to have gold fever. Plans are being made for a big mining expedition in the spring. They want to go to a spot in the mountains where George has previously staked some gold claims. Excitement is high and if all goes as planned, we'll all be rich by this time next year.

Ted's 243 rifle blew up in his face the other day. A friend had given him some reloaded shells to use and when he pulled the trigger they exploded. He was lucky that all that happened to him was powder burned eye balls and a good scare. We'll buy our shells from now on thank you! That was Ted's big scare, now for mine.

Finally, we've gotten around to building our outhouse. I am overjoyed with the thought of finally getting it done. While helping Ted rip boards lengthwise with a chain saw, Ted told me to grab hold of the boards and pull them towards myself while he cut them. While reaching for a better grip I grabbed the chain saw instead of the board. Imagine my surprise when I felt the chain cutting away. I pulled my hand back instantly but was sure that some of my fingers were missing. So, like any smart person would do, I stuck my hand behind my back instead of looking at it. I guess I was hoping that if I didn't look it would just go away. About that time Ted looked up to see what I was doing and said my face was all eyes and as white as a sheet. He grabbed my hand from behind my back to see what was wrong, and much to my surprise, it wasn't even bleeding. There were three little nicks in the skin that weren't even deep enough to bleed. Since then the chain saw and I have parted company.

Chapter 6

An Abundance of Wildlife

Hi there,

Wow, it's September already.

One of the sled dogs broke its chain the other day and tangled with a porcupine. It was quite the job getting all of the quills out. The inside of its throat and mouth were both white with quills. As the dog was half wild to start with and didn't want anyone near it, the men had to run the dog around a tree until it hit the end of it's chain, then push him a little bit farther until he was almost unconscious, then pulled the quills out while he was in a more docile state of mind.

Ted and a friend just returned from a backpack trip up Hitchcock Mountain. I decided to stay home this time and let the guys go. They had a good trip and enjoyed getting away, but were glad to get home again too as it was really cold higher up. When they woke up in the morning, there was a solid layer of ice on the inside of the nylon tent where the condensation from their breath had frozen solid. They had their tent set up on the edge of Black Lake, at an altitude of roughly three-thousand feet. It's a picturesque spot with the lake nestled in a small valley amid tall pines and rolling grassy hillsides. Early in the morning as they lay in the tent they watched a moose feeding and wading around in the water nearby. Afternoons were spent climbing around on the hillsides high above the camp. They would spend hours sitting and glassing the surrounding hillsides for sheep. One afternoon while sitting and glassing they saw thirty sheep, none big enough to shoot, thirteen moose, four black bear, one wolverine, and six caribou. As they sat relaxing and enjoying this rare opportunity to study the abundance of wildlife around them, they were lucky enough to be able to watch a cow moose teaching her calf how to respond to her danger signal. When the calf didn't listen, she would chase it into the water and would thrash it thoroughly until it figured out that this was what it was supposed to be doing when she gave a danger signal. How fortunate they were to have been able to share this special moment of nature. They came home empty handed but refreshed and totally at peace within.

Last night the dogs howled most of the night again and we could hear a pack of wolves howling down by the dog houses. One night a wolf tried to pull one of the sled dogs out of its house by its tail and ended up pulling half of its tail off. The dog was cut up quite badly. The neighbors lead sled dog lost an eye to wolves while chained to its house one night. They can do a lot of damage in a short time if they aren't scared off.

Ted, George and Robin are across the lake on a big hunting trip. Robin, George's son-in-law is visiting from Alberta. I'm glad Ted has a chance to get away for a few days to relax and enjoy his good friends. It will be a most welcome break for him from getting the winters wood in I'm sure. I must close now but will add more at a later date.

Sept. 11, 1981

Hi again! The men returned from their hunting trip across the lake safe and sound. All they came home with was one goat, although a cow moose almost stepped on the tent while they slept one night. It poured rain the entire time they were away and was extremely windy too. Because of the wind they were stranded on the far side of the lake for 3 extra days until the lake calmed down enough for them to cross it. Atlin Lake can go from dead calm to five foot waves in a matter of minutes.

When they finally did cross, they were still in four foot waves. They ran out of food except for some old pancake mix that wouldn't rise so for the last three days of the trip they ate flat pancakes. They were three wet, cold and hungry boys when they did finally make it home. You wouldn't believe the junk they brought home with them! While camped on the far side of the lake, they found a couple of old cabins and collected a lot of what they call treasures. They even hauled home part of and old burned out tin stove. One thing they brought home that was interesting was a rock that in years past was used to grind grain in. You can see where it's worn hollow in the center from the grinding.

I have a pure white puppy now from two of Holly's sled dogs. I'll be looking after another pure white pup from the same litter as mine while its owners are in hunting camp. We named our pup Casper. His father's name is Ghost so that makes him Casper, Son of Ghost. He looks like a little polar bear cub with his black button eyes and nose. The pups are so much company and I'm having lots of fun with them. Today I took them for a walk in the bush behind our cabin. They have so much energy that I decided to run with them. I set off running with one leash in each hand when all of a sudden both pups stopped dead right in front of me and down I went flat on my face. They decided that this was lots of fun and licked me half to death before I was able to regain both my breath and my feet. No more running for us, from now on we'll just walk sedately along.

I fried up a rabbit the other night for Goldy. She couldn't tell the difference between the rabbit and the chicken they were having for supper. We always have a pot of stew or soup simmering on the top of the wood stove. The smell permeates every corner of the cabin making one constantly hungry and the fire keeps the cabin snug and warm.

It's time to think about getting our winter's meat in, so Ted and I took another stab at backpacking up Hitchcock Mountain moose hunting. This time it started to pour half way to the top making the huge rocks really slippery. In a small valley near the top we huddled under a bushy tree and ate our lunch. We kept hoping the rain would stop but as it hadn't even slowed down by the time we finished we pushed on in the downpour towards our goal. Our arrival at scenic Black Lake and the setting up of our camp took every bit of energy we had left and before long we crawled gratefully into our sleeping bags and drifted off to sleep listening to the sound of the rain on the nylon tent. Towards morning something woke me and as I lay listening to the stillness surrounding us, once again I heard a noise. (I have developed into an extremely light sleeper when not protected by the cabins walls.) Shaking Ted awake and signaling him to be quiet we both lay listening when all of a sudden we realized we were about to get stepped on by a moose. Ted gave a yell that startled the moose. The moose took off running straight towards the lake. Before long we heard her jump into the water and managed to struggle out of our sleeping bags just in time to watch her swimming across the lake. During the night the rain had turned into snow. We set off to investigate our surroundings and look for any other moose sign. Realizing the only fresh sign around was from the moose we had spooked earlier, we decided to head home. Following an old overgrown rock slide down the mountainside saved us some time but was hard going. In some places we literally had to crawl on our hands and

knees through willows and brush. Not ⎵
with big heavy, bulky packs on our backs.
sure glad to reach the bottom.

Sept. 17
Ted and George are working hard trying to finish off the inside of George's house. Since its rained every day so far in September, it's getting awfully damp in the camper. They'll appreciate finally being able to move in. I know we did and can't imagine how we lived in our camper as long as we did.

Ted and I baked bread in the wood stove for the first time the other day. It took the two of us to figure out how to regulate the oven. The bread actually turned out not too bad. Ted is always more than willing to help me out.

The two pups are growing like mad and both like to sleep on the roof of the dog house Ted built for them.

A few of the mountains have snow on them already and are surely pretty with a dusting of white. We had a heavy frost last night and the meadow in front of the cabin was white until about ten-thirty this morning. The fall colors are gorgeous and the mountains and meadows are a sight to see. I have five rolls of film ready to be developed.

We picked some wild mushrooms the other day. What a treat! I made mushroom rice and we had fresh grouse with it. It was George and Goldys forty-fifth anniversary so I had them over for dinner. Everything was delicious.

Getting the winter's wood in has been hard on us both and we ache all over.

Time to say good-bye again but will try and write again soon.

October 13

Well, here it is the middle of October already. Yesterday was George's 66 birthday as well as Thanksgiving. We tried to buy a turkey in Atlin to celebrate but there wasn't one to be found at our one and only store. We ended up with a big chicken instead and enjoyed it just as much. Hope everyone there is fine and that you think of us while you are all together for Thanksgiving.

The guys left at first light Thanksgiving Day to go moose hunting. They arrived home with seven grouse but no moose. Dick and Holly flew us out some moose meat from hunting camp this week. We've really been enjoying it. Now that the price of meat is so high most of the hunters take all of the meat home with them when they leave. The meat Dick sent us had been claimed by a grizzly bear and then buried by the bear so the hunter didn't want anything to do with it. Lucky us!

The hunter had shot the moose on the first day of his hunt. When they went to get the meat and bring it back into camp a grizzly had claimed the meat and was in the process of burying it. As the guide had a grizzly hunter with them, he shot the bear but unfortunately just wounded it. They then had to track the wounded bear and finally came across it just as it was getting dark. The bear was one of the largest shot in this area in recent years. From it's head to it's tail it measured eight feet four inches long.

There are quite a few grizzlies in this area and on one of our hikes we discovered some huge grizzly bear tracks. Ted had size twelve gum boots on and when he stood inside the bears track he didn't come close to filling them.

The sunrises and sunsets are magnificent this time of year. It doesn't get light until around eight thirty or so and is dark again around seven. It's seven a.m. right now and I'm waiting for it to get light enough outside so I can see to do the laundry.

Laundry was done in a tin wash tub with a bar of sunlight soap. It saved a lot of mess when done outside so that's where I usually ended up doing it. I would set up the square tin laundry tub on a big stump close to the cabin, pour in the ice cold water that had been hauled in five gallon buckets from the creek a good half mile away. Since it was October, it was painfully cold on the hands so frequent trips were made inside to warm them. Laundry was the most detested chore there was and often my hands would crack open and bleed when I bent my fingers.

Ted hooked up our wood heat stove the other day as we were freezing to death. We didn't have enough stovepipe for both the heat stove and the cook stove so we had to disconnect the cook stove. This means no more oven and no more nice fresh bread. It's back to Bannoch for us. Just when we finally got the oven figured out! Bannoch is a fried indian bread that the Natives make that consists of flour, brown sugar, baking powder, salt, and butter or lard. Sometimes berries are added to the mixture. This in years past was a most important part of the Native diet.

I've ordered Ted a pair of nice warm slippers and a pair of insulated socks out of the Sears Catalogue. He needs something warm on his feet as he's outside so much of the time. I'd like to order him a warm housecoat for Christmas but we'll have to wait and see what the money situation is like. He gets bits and pieces of work at a small sawmill not too far away.

Goldy and I went into Atlin today and while there we decided to check at the float plane dock to see if there were any messages from hunting camp for us. Good thing we checked as the pilots wife had been kept busy fighting dogs off of the three moose that had been sent out of camp for us. What a shock for two women to have three large moose dumped into their laps all at once. Along with the moose came a note from Dick saying that they would probably be flying out more meat to us the next week as they had a hunter in camp that didn't want to take any meat home. As it turned out he shot a caribou so we had a nice variety of meat for the winter. We were mighty thankful that now there was enough food to see everyone through the winter. What a great feeling.

The biggest problem we had at the moment was what in the world were we going to do with all this meat so it didn't spoil. George had a small freezer in Atlin that he kept at a friends and it wouldn't come close to holding it all. As things turned out we lucked out again and were able to buy a small freezer that someone had ordered through the Sears Catalogue and then decided they couldn't afford upon its arrival in Atlin. Due to the cost of the freight to ship it back we were able to buy it cheap! Even with the price reduced we still didn't have enough money to buy it so Dick and Holly went halves on it with us. We were able to pay someone in town five dollars a month to cover the electricity that it used and kept it at their place.

So far today we've canned four dozen pints and three dozen quarts of meat and there's a lot left to do.

Right now Ted is sitting at the front window counting squirrels. Their pelts are worth about two dollars each right now. The other day while looking out the window, Taku, the sled dog that caught his own fish, ran past with a rabbit in his mouth.

I've done nothing but can moose for the last few days. I've canned well over two hundred pints. What a job! I'll be quite happy if I never see another canner.

Dick and Holly arrived home from hunting camp this morning with lots of stories to tell. We were glad to see them. It will mean a lot less work for us now that we don't have the dogs and horses to feed.

We're still busy, busy, cutting up meat. There's raw meat everywhere yuck!

We had a half an inch of snow yesterday. The ground looks so clean and white and is sparkling like diamonds. The mountains are beautiful all blanketed in white. It won't be long now until winter sets in for real.

We had a chimney fire this morning so Ted's on the roof right now rattling a chain down the pipe to knock the creosote down. What a messy job! George, Goldy, Ted and I went to Dick and Holly's for dinner last night and had wheat berries and lynx. Not your everyday cuisine. George and I liked the lynx and found it to be a lot like pork tenderloin. I didn't think much of the wheat berries. Ted and Goldy had a hard time eating a member of the cat family but didn't mind the wheat. It's getting cold and snows almost every day now. The other day Ted and I backpacked into Carter Mountain behind our cabin. I really wasn't too sure if I was going to make it home again or not. When we did finally get home I could hardly wait to jump in bed and as I neared the top of the ladder to the loft I stubbed my second toe and broke it. Ouch! For the last two days not only has my toe been sore but the muscles in the back of my legs have been so sore I haven't strayed far from the bed. Ted's muscles are in the same shape as mine so we make a dandy pair.

Dick got the pictures back of the grizzly we got the moose meat from, boy was it ever huge! I hope I never run into one in my travels as I'm sure I'd die of fright.

You asked in your last letter what we wanted for Christmas. You also asked what furniture we have now. As far as furniture goes, we're pretty well set. We have a rickety old wooden table and chairs that we bought off of a school teacher in Carcross, Yukon. She was being transferred back to Montreal and wouldn't be needing them anymore. The table is not very sturdy but will do until we can cut some more boards and get our breakfast nook finished. In the living room we have a couch that George picked up for one dollar at an auction in Alberta. He paid the dollar and then hauled it all the way up here for us. Also, a friend loaned us a big chair that they weren't using. We sleep on a foamy on the floor of the loft, and keep our clothing in one trunk. Actually we're quite comfortable. Not classy but comfortable. I'll tell you what we could use if you can find one reasonable enough and that's a transistor radio. I'm going nuts with no music in my life. Another thing we need desperately is a flashlight. We can never find the outhouse in the dark and it's getting to be a real problem as it's dark most of the time now. We could use warm socks or flannel shirts too. Hope this gives you some ideas.

Our days were getting shorter now and during the darkest months we had to keep an oil lamp lit all but a couple of hours a day. The temperatures dropped as low as minus forty degrees Fahrenheit during the winter but we were content and cozy in our little log cabin. We appreciated all the food we had worked so hard to put away.

We found the biggest mistake we had made while building the cabin was that we put the sleeping loft over the kitchen where the wood stove was located. No matter what the outside temperature was or how cool it was downstairs, one just about died of heat in the loft. It got so bad as the winter progressed that we had to cut a hole in the logs above the bed with a chain saw to let some of the heat out. We put a small window in the hole but the window was never closed even at 40 below. We had it all figured out that if we left anything on the main floor of the cabin, the floor would act as a freezer, the first step to the loft made a great cooler and so on. This system worked perfectly for us once we figured it out.

George and Goldy had gone south for the winter and we missed them terribly. We spent many hours playing cards, chess, checkers and backgammon together. We did a lot of reading and spent many hours outside taking long walks in the crisp, sparkling snow. Our trips to town were few and far between this time of year as in order to start the pick up we had to put red hot coals out of the wood stove, into a five gallon metal pail and then set the pail under the truck. This process had to be repeated until the truck would start and all the parts were thawed enough to move The battery was kept inside the cabin and had the place of honor beside the wood stove so it wouldn't freeze and break. Getting the truck running was such a chore that we only did it when absolutely necessary.

By the time spring finally arrived we were more than ready for it.

Chapter 7

Spring

April 28, 1981,
Although its still winter here it feels more like spring every day. Our temperatures have been as high as plus forty so far. There's still about two feet of snow in the bush but the roads are all mud again. There is a saying in this country that goes like this, "In this country we have nine months of winter and three of poor sledding." Right now there's mud everywhere!

We aren't able to do laundry or have a decent bath as clean water is hard to come by with the creeks and rivers all swollen with run off. Think of us when you turn on your tap, or climb into a hot steamy tub for a long relaxing soak.

There's a lot of wildlife around this spring, probably because of all the snows still in the high country. We've had a couple of caribou hanging around the cabin lately. One day we were lucky enough to see a cow moose that had moments before given birth to her wobbly legged little calf at the end of our lane. The calf was so new it hadn't figured out how to stand yet. Where there's lots of wildlife, there's lots of wolves, and they are plentiful. We hear them often especially at night.

The Gray Jays, called Whisky Jacks in the North, helped keep us amused. Magpies and Pine Grosbeaks were plentiful. One day we watched as a Magpie grabbed hold of Holly's cat's tail and tried to drag it away from its food dish so that the bird could eat the food. We often saw lynx tracks close to the cabin in the snow. There were lots of squirrels around.

We had a huge horned owl and three young ones living a short distance from the cabin. During the night they would hunt from the cabin roof directly above our heads. Their claws tick, tick, ticked, as they paced back and forth on the peak searching for the smallest movement on the ground below. Whenever we ventured up the laneway, Momma and all three babies were usually perched on the log fence rails keeping an eye on us.

Porcupines were plentiful. I got some great pictures of a baby one that was up a small tree by the cabin. The dogs were constantly full of quills and once the same dog had quills in him four times in the same day.

```
We made seventy-eight bottles of Root Beer this
morning. Now comes the tricky part. It has to sit
quietly in a warm dark place for five to seven days
before we can drink it. We usually wrap it in
blankets and set it in the loft. That seems to work
pretty well for us unless the temperature fluctu-
ates and the bottles decide to explode. One night
we had just gotten nicely to sleep, when suddenly,
it sounded like firecrackers going off all around
us, scaring the life out of us until we figured out
what all the noise was about. What a mess! Sticky
Root Beer all over the loft and the blankets. The
next morning we had to pull out the wash tub, haul
water from the creek and clean up the mess. Even
the simple things one does up here can sometimes
turn into major undertakings.
```

Ted hadn't had any work at all since December and, as it was now June, the bank decided that it wanted our old pick up truck back. This was devastating news. When we'd come north, we had brought with us our two handmade saddles. We'd left our quarter horse and her stud colt on a large hay ranch in the Chilcotin Country of central B.C. but we figured the saddles might just come in handy. I must clarify the point that although we had a horse, I still was the world's worst rider. I was so scared I froze every time the horse moved. Anyway, we figured it was far more important to keep the truck than the saddles at this point so Ted took them into town to try and sell them. The problem with this idea was that although most people would have liked them, no one else had any money either.

Finally, a neighbor took pity on us and put us to work building rail fences and doing odd jobs for him. He advanced us the five hundred dollars that we needed to pay our truck off. What a relief it was to have that threat gone, for without the truck Ted had no chance of getting to and from a job even if he was lucky enough to find one.

```
We've been enjoying the nice weather we've been
having but there's black flies and mosquitoes ev-
erywhere. We notice it more than usual right now as
we've been busy building a rail fence for a neigh-
bor. This is not a fun job! We've put up just about
a mile of fence so far this last week. At night we
have a hard time dragging ourselves home and climbing
the ladder to the loft to bed. You'd think my poor
old body would get used to all of this punishment
and would stop hurting so much but no such luck.
This is definitely a man's world and at times like
this I still can't seem to figure out if I'm having
fun yet or not. When we do get finished with the
fence, we have gates to build for his Morgan horse
stud pens. Then, we have the outside of a mobile
home and outhouse to paint. After we're finished
with all of that we have more fences to build. The
style of fences we are building take a lot of extra
work but are safe for the wildlife as they're not
likely to hurt themselves trying to jump them.
     We had an interview in town with an outfitter
about work in hunting camp for both Ted and myself
this fall. Ted would be guiding big game hunters
and I would be the trail cook. We have our fingers
crossed that this will work out but we won't know
for a while yet.
     Keith, one of our friends recently decided to
leave the North for Victoria. He gave us some most
welcomed gifts today. He gave me his scrub board
```

with a wringer attached. Imagine not having to wring all the clothing out by hand on laundry day. I'm thrilled as you'll never know how much work this will save me. He also gave us the frame off of his brass bed. We'll attach it to plywood and for the first time in over a year be up off the floor to sleep. It will be wonderful I'm sure. Last but not least, we inherited his full size galvanized bath tub. I can't imagine submerging all of myself in warm water at the same time, I'm sure we won't even mind hauling the extra water for this luxury.

By this time, we had graduated from our baths in the dishpan to bathing in the square laundry tub that we had picked up on one of our rare trips to Whitehorse. On a nice day we would set the tub outside in a grassy little wildflower-covered meadow that was surrounded by poplar trees and climb in. Ted looked really silly sitting in this little tub with his knees up around his ears, while I poured water over his head so he could wash his hair. We had many good laughs and took some very cute pictures of all the goings on.

It's been really dry so far this year and the forest fire danger is high. We both love the fifteen or sixteen hours of light that we have a day. A person can accomplish so much this time of year with so much daylight.

Today we found out we both got jobs in hunting camp for the fall. We're really excited and are looking forward to this new experience. Ted has been reading Outdoor Life magazines and books on hunting and fishing since he's been old enough to read and his dream has always been to live in the mountains where he could hunt, fish, trap and fly. Making a living while living his dream will be a bonus.

We still haven't heard anything definite from the government regarding the land we have staked. They sure are taking their time.

Ted's been busy shoeing the horses and getting them ready for hunting camp. He learned how to shoe from Arnold. Arnold is the person we built the fences for. I know all of the new things he's learning will come in handy once we get into the remote mountain country where the camps are located. One thing I've learned from watching the men is that there's quite an art to shoeing a horse, especially one that doesn't want to be shod. We've had lots of good laughs lately watching the men trying to get the shoes on and I have some great pictures of the proceedings.

Chapter 8

Peace and Solitude

This weekend George, Goldy, Ted and I are planning a week long boat trip. We're heading down to the south end of Atlin Lake. We'll go through Torries Channel to the Llewellan Ice Fields. The Llewellan Glacier is part of the Juneau Ice Fields that feed Atlin Lake which is the headwaters of the Yukon River. Atlin lake is roughly one hundred miles long with about twenty miles of it in the Yukon. It is the largest freshwater Lake in British Columbia. Teresa island, in Atlin lake is the highest point of land surrounded by fresh water in the world. The island itself is about fifteen miles long and three miles across. The government has set aside this island as a provincial park to protect wildlife.

The scenery in this area is spectacular and is some of the prettiest anywhere in the world. We are looking forward to our trip and hope the weather holds until we can get across the lake and into the channel where it's protected from the wind.

The reflections in the milky glacier water of the channel are breathtakingly beautiful, and bring with them a special kind of awe and a thankfulness at being able to have shared in this beauty and to have refreshed ones soul.

July 22

As you can see I wasn't able to get this in the mail before we left on our boat trip so I'll add to it now.

We enjoyed our trip tremendously and all returned totally refreshed and at peace within. The trout fishing was excellent and the weather was exceptionally nice. I'll make sure we send you some pictures. The area we were in was unbelievably remote, picturesque and rugged. The half mile wide channel flows gently, winding it's way through stately majestic, snow capped mountains. Pathways of long forgotten slides scar the mountainsides as they leave rocky trails in the virgin timber. High above tree line, meadows of vivid alpine green are visible. Higher yet amid the snow capped peaks, mountain goats can sometimes be seen from the boat. Waterfalls and run-off streams abound.

Hundreds of tiny islands dot the channel, some make perfect camping spots. Wildlife abounds. We were lucky enough to have a moose swim across the channel close to our boat. What a majestic animal and how exciting it was to see him in his natural environment. A powerful swimmer for sure. We watched a bear as he swam from one island to the next, his blue black hair glistening in the sunlight.

Goldy and I investigated a large glacier cave with a crystal clear run off stream trickling through it. Subdued sunlight filtered eerily through the ice. Along the grassy edges of the stream wildflowers bloomed in a profusion of colors.

Ted got his gold pan out of the boat and climbing high above the cave tried his luck at gold panning at the foot of a huge waterfalls. George, fishing off the edge of the ice, caught a nice lake trout in no time at all.

Who could ever ask for more out of life than to experience the wondrous beauty, peace and solitude of this remote little piece of heaven. Years later when my parents visited us from Vancouver, we were fortunate to have been able to share the peacefulness of this area with them. We enjoyed our time together fishing and soaking up the unsurpassed beauty of our surroundings.

Chapter 9

Pack Strings and Rodeos

June 30, 1982

Hi! It's me again,

The pack string of gentle horses that we rented for this hunting season arrived on schedule and did we ever get a big surprise! It turned out that just about every one of them had never been packed, shod or ridden. The few that had been used in the past hadn't been handled in years. They had all been running wild on the many miles of open range land in northern Alberta. This was a big shock to all concerned as we thought we had rented a well broken, gentle pack string of horses suitable for greenhorn hunters to ride. This should be an interesting season filled with many surprises to say the least. Personally, I'm shaking in my boots at the thought of riding one of these horses never mind trusting my life to one. I am not what one would call an accomplished rider and can always be counted on to provide everyone with their daily entertainment. Oh well at least I keep everyone laughing.

The first thing we did was shoe some of the horses. This was far easier said than done. Next, all of them had to have either pack saddles and pack boxes called panniers or riding saddles put on them. A difficult chore to say the least. With this job finally accomplished, the horses then had to be trailed sixty miles through town, across rapidly flowing rivers, canyons, valleys, bottomless bogs, and along rugged mountain trails into one of the hunting base camps where they would be used in the upcoming season.

Ted and four other men spent from seven a.m. to five p.m. putting the saddles on the horses. Then, the whole situation worsened and things turned into a wild west show. I'm sure I could have made a fortune if I had been smart enough to sell tickets. At five p.m., with the horses finally ready, the guides and wranglers headed out through town and down the trail towards camp. Total confusion reigned the result being sixty miles of rodeo. The towns people lined up along the road to laugh at them as they passed by. Trying to keep the horses in the ditches until they were out of town was impossible, and before a mile had passed packs and gear already needed to be adjusted.

The next excitement arose at Pine Creek as the men tried to trail the green horses across the wooden deck of the bridge that spans the rapidly rushing Pine creek below them. The horses refused to cooperate at all and the sounds of their hooves on the wooden bridge deck spooked them so bad that they would not move at all. The only other way across the river was for the men and horses to ford the river. Ted's horse lost it's footing in the rapidly moving water and by the time it righted itself, Ted was soaking wet but not hurt. The river at this point was only about four feet deep but was fast and mighty cold with a large waterfall only a short distance below where they were crossing. The pack string of green horses decided that they weren't going to cross the river under any circumstances so the men had to hook them to the saddle horns on the horses they were riding and pull them across. Keep in mind that the horses they were pulling with were just as wild as the ones they were pulling. What a job it was for sure! Finally, everyone arrived on the far shore safe and sound, the saddles and tack were reorganized, and once again they were off. They had only gotten about two miles under their belts when some unknown thing spooked the horses and they were off again on another wild ride with all the horses trying to go in different directions at the same time. While all this excitement was happening Ted's horse decided that it didn't want Ted on his back anymore and reared up on his hind legs trying to get rid of him. The horse was pulled right over backwards by the other spooking horses. Ted felt the horse under him going and managed to jump clear all except his one foot that is. He had a mighty sore foot for quite a while afterwards. The men persevered and kept on riding until eleven. p.m. By that time all were cranky and tempers were short so they decided to set up camp for the night at Rose Creek cabin, a dilapidated weathered board falling down miners cabin in the twenty mile long Blue Canyon. This valley was heavily mined during the Klondike gold rush and remnants of days past were evident in the scarred ground everywhere one looked.

Setting up camp is a big job at the best of times and was only made worse this night by the wild horses the cranky men, and Ted's sore foot. The one thing they had going for them was that the horses were as tired as the men. Once the horses had been staked out or hobbled for the night, watered and fed, it was time for the men to grab a snack and fall thankfully into their bedrolls. This night bed consisted of a sleeping bag rolled out on the louse infested rotting board floor of the dilapidated cabin.

Morning came early and they were off again as soon as they had gotten all the gear reorganized. No small chore under the circumstances! After another day of pack strings, rodeos, and short tempers Line Lake Camp was a most welcome sight. Gratefully the men turned the horses over to the waiting wranglers.

Line Lake Camp is the hunting camp located closest to the town of Atlin and sits at an altitude of about three thousand feet. Because it is the closest to town it gets used the heaviest during hunting season. The lake itself is one in a series of lakes and rivers that make up the Gladys drainage system. The camp is located on the edge of a crystal clear lake ringed by majestic mountains. The camp sits nestled in a buck brush covered meadow on one end of the lake and consists of four log cabins of various ages, four tent frames, a corral made of logs and a falling down log lean-to that's used as a tack shed along with a smoke house and board out house. Along one side of the camp runs a river that joins Line and Eva lakes together. At the opposite end of the lake is another river that joins Line and Angel lakes together. There is good fishing in both of the rivers and all of the lakes.

The Trout fishing is great in the river beside the camp. One of the hunters caught a twenty seven pound Lake Trout in the river one afternoon casting out off of the shore. In the river at the far end of the lake there is excellent Greyling fishing and a person can catch a fish with almost every cast, a lot of them either record book or near record book size.

The evening after the men's arrival the Beaver float plane arrived to take Ted back to town. The others would be staying in that camp for the rest of the season. Ted being nuts over airplanes, found the last few days well worth while as he got to fly the Beaver part of the way home.

Once at home he was extremely sore for a few days as he was using muscles that hadn't been used in two years since the last time he had been on a horse.

Before we head into camp for good we have to get our winters fire wood in. There will be snow on the ground by the time we come out.

August 10, 1982

As things turned out, not only did we have time to get our wood in but Ted also found enough time to go sheep hunting. He and the teenage son of a friend, left this morning and plan on climbing up Hitchcock Mountain and then will camp at Black Lake for a few days. I hope he gets a sheep as it's a long hard climb to the mountains top especially with a heavy pack on your back.

Well it's now the next morning and believe it or not, Ted returned late yesterday with a nice ram roughly one inch over a full curl. Sheep must be eight years old or have a full curl to be legal to shoot. By the sound of things they had quite a trip and are both pretty tired. I don't know many people who can leave home in the morning, climb a mountain, and return home late the same day with a nice sheep. The meat will be a most welcome change this winter.

Shortly after this we were on our way into camp and on our way towards another new adventure

Chapter 10

Hunting Camp

Hunting season had finally started, and while Ted took out his first backpack sheep hunters, a husband and wife team from Utah, I stayed in town to help out at the lodge. The Beaver float plane dropped Ted and the hunters off on Tern Lake, a puddle sized lake at the head of Tern Creek in the Snowden Mountains. The lake is so small that it takes a good, experienced pilot to land and take off of it. From Tern Creek they hiked throughout the mountains setting up camps in the evening where ever they were at the time. They didn't get a sheep on this trip but had a great time playing hide and seek with one.

One day while the men went out hunting the hunter's wife decided to stay in camp and relax. While resting she saw a nice size black ram run right through the middle of the camp. The same ram sat on a rock high on the mountainside every morning and watched them as the ate their breakfast and got ready for the days hunt. Once they were lucky enough to get within seventeen feet of a three quarter curl ram but as he wasn't big enough to shoot, they took pictures of him instead. I can hardly wait to see the pictures as it's not every day one gets that close to a wild sheep, illusive creatures that they are.

August 25, 1982
We arrived in camp yesterday. I enjoyed the flight in the Beaver float plane but was nervous as usual. The pilot is one of the best bush pilots in the North but as he is in the last stages of

emphysema coughs constantly and always has a cigarette hanging out of his mouth.

There are lots of up and down drafts when flying in the mountains and the flight as usual was pretty rough. It seems that every time we fly anywhere my seat disappears and I end up having to sit on top of a rutting, stinky old moose or crammed into a corner with my nose pressed up against a window so that there's more room for gear etc. For some unknown reason Ted always seems to get a nice comfortable front seat with a perfect view of our surroundings.

The flight into camp was beautiful as we flew over miles of remote mountains, valleys full of first growth timber, rapidly rushing rivers, river canyons and waterfalls. The scenery was spectacular and the flight gave us a good idea of just how remote our location actually would be for the next while. No running to the store if we run out of anything or no running to the Doctor if the need arises. We are now on our own and totally cut off from the life style we are accustomed to.

This camp is the newest one in the hunting area and is the most isolated camp. Because of this, it is still really primitive. There are no cabins here just tent frames and wall tents. The cook tent has a wood floor and log two and a half foot walls that are chinked with moss. Inside the tent is a small tin stove with an oven in it, called a Yukon stove. There is a ten foot table made out of weathered boards and some rather primitive board shelving. The boards were flown in attached to the floats on the Beaver aircraft.

Not far from the cook tent is an old canvas tent framed with logs, that is used as a supply tent. This tent is so old that parts of it are held together with rusty safety pins. One hundred feet from this on the other side of a small crystal clear bubbling glacier fed creek are two canvas wall tents that are set up for sleeping. Inside each tent is a small tin pop-up wood stove that is used for heat during the cold nights. Dry Lake Camp

Are We Having Fun Yet?

is nestled in a deep valley, and is on t
a small lake that sits just at tree line

This camp will be our new home for the
weeks. We aren't sure how long we'll be able to
stay here as the lake is pretty shallow this year
and the float plane is already having trouble taking off and landing on it. We are sitting fairly
high up in the mountains here, about 3500 feet, and
the lake has a couple of volcanic vents in it's
bottom. The vents usually stay frozen solid but if
the year turns out to be exceptionally warm, the
ice in the holes melt and all the water drains out
of the lake. Every five years or so the lake goes
dry, hence the name Dry Lake. The lake is emptying
at a rate of about a foot a day right now. It's
quite picturesque as each level leaves a ring in
the shoreline at the edge of the lake. The shoreline is marked with dozens of rings and is an
unusual sight for sure.

Ted enjoys the guiding and loves all the mountain climbing and horseback riding that it involves. Sometimes I get to go out for the day with
the men but not as often as I'd like to. I'm
usually too busy cooking, baking and doing every
ones laundry.

We do get lots of flying in flying from camp to
camp and loving flying as much as Ted does, he is
in his glory. I'm getting used to it but know I'll
never love flying like Ted does.

Most of our sheep hunters have been lucky and
have been able to get a sheep. We have a goat
hunter in camp right now who is happy as he has
already gotten a nice sheep. We are expecting new
hunters in on Friday if the weather holds so the
plane can get in. So much depends on air travel in
this isolated area.

The guides haven't seen much grizzly sign yet.
That's just fine with me as I'm in camp alone so
much of the time. I keep a shot gun with me at all
times and have it loaded with s.s.g's then slugs
then s.s.g's etc. I'll be here alone at night some
times but not too often I hope. Just the thought of

it scares me half to death.

Ted and one of the native guides are working hard cutting a trail into the Nakina River country. This is a rugged, remote area with lots of almost impassable trails that have been used only by the animals since the natives and odd trapper used them at the turn of the century. I have my fingers crossed that they are able to make it back to camp tonight as I'm certainly far from the bravest person in the world especially alone on a mountain in the dark.

Well, I'm glad to report that the men made it back into camp late last night. On the way back they spotted two different size sets of grizzly tracks both fairly close to camp. I'm glad I didn't know they were there while I was alone in the dark. Like the old saying goes, ignorance is bliss.

There are a lot of Arctic ground squirrels in this area. They have no fear of anything or anybody and will destroy what ever they can reach in short order. On Ted's last hunt one sat on his head while he was sleeping under a tree. His hunters got a real laugh out of that.

Must run as I have bread to bake yet before the men get back to camp. The hardest part of making bread out here in a tent is trying to get the dough to rise. I usually throw in double the yeast that is called for and hold my breath that it rises. I've had pretty good luck so far.

There's a plane due in next week so I'll send this letter out then with the pilot to be mailed.

The bush pilots were our saving grace. They ran all kinds of errands and did all kinds of favors for us during our months in the bush. We were always glad to see them and catch up on all the news from the outside world.

September 2

Hi again. Thought I'd fill you in on what's been happening around here while I finally have a few moments to myself.

Having four hunters in camp has been keeping us all busy. Our new hunters are from Florida and we've had lots of fun with them for sure. Let me tell you they sure can eat! Must be all the fresh air and exercise that makes them so hungry. They will be heading out tomorrow as their hunt is finished. I was really surprised when they gave me over one hundred dollars in tips for cooking. Ted got a nice tip from them too. He usually gets one hundred dollars for each animal the hunters shoot These two hunters got two nice goat while here and also got two exceptionally beautiful caribou and a big moose. In this area we have the Alaska Yukon moose and they are the largest moose in the world. They are a lot bigger than the moose farther south.

Speaking of moose, a cow moose swam across the lake in front of the cook tent the other day. I should have some good pictures of her as I put the big zoom lens on. We are enjoying our camera and are thankfull that we have a good one with a great variety of lenses.

We just found out that the husband and wife team of back pack sheep hunters that Ted had out earlier in the season, enjoyed their trip so much they rebooked again for later in the season on the condition that Ted guides them. They didn't get a sheep on the first hunt but said the trip had been well worth while just to have Ted get them to within seventeen feet of a three quarter curl ram. The funny part of this story is that although they didn't know it, there was another guide with two hunters watching them through a spotting scope. Their guide had a lot of problems with the hunters after this as they both wanted Ted to guide them. Once they shot a nice sheep of their own they were more than content with their own native guide.

The moose that our last hunters shot was shot in the lake. The men tried pulling it out of the water using two of our biggest pack horses but the moose was so large that the horses couldn't budge it. It took the men eight hours of back breaking work to cape out the moose. It took them that long to skin out the head and neck etc. as they were working in the ice cold water the entire time. They finally arrived back in camp around four thirty a.m. and I was sure glad to see them as I had no idea where they were and had been trying to keep supper warm for them. By the time they finally did show up I was convinced that every little sound I heard was a grizzly bear that was just waiting to get me. I had lit the Coleman lantern while I waited and sat in the cook tent reading and trying to keep the food warm. I was too scared to leave that tent and go to my own tent as when it's dark in the mountains it's really dark! I didn't realize it but the lantern lit the tent up like a beacon and the men told me they could tell the exact moment that I heard them coming down the trail into camp. They watched as my silhouette moved slowly across the tent to grab my shotgun. You never heard such noise in your life as they made then. From that night on until the end of hunting season no one neared our camp in the dark without making a big racket.

When finally they did arrive back in camp everyone was soaking wet, cranky and hungry. The meal was gulped down in silence and dry clothing put on. By then it was light enough to pack up the horses and head back out again to bring in the meat.

Luckily, one of the hunters turned out to be a butcher by trade and not only did his help speed up the butchering process he took the time to give Ted a lesson on the easiest way to butcher a moose. It sure simplifies things when you know what you're doing.

Again will close and try and send this out on the next plane.

Hello! Here it is the middle of September already. The plane has come and gone taking our Florida hunters with it. We have enough meat in camp right at the moment to sink a battle ship. Ted and I are alone in camp and are enjoying a well earned rest. Right now we have the meat from two caribou, a side of bacon and some chickens that the plane dropped off when it picked up the hunters, I have a caribou roast of at least 10 pounds in the oven cooking for tonight's supper. It's either feast or famine this far from civilization. Caribou is one of my favorite meats but one must be careful when preparing it. You must first inspect the meat thoroughly and pick out the warble eggs that the fly's lay along the back strap under the skin. Caribou are always loaded with them.

Ted is gaining weight and soon won't fit into his clothing if he isn't careful. He's been eating four large meals a day plus snacks. I'm sure it's all the crisp, fresh, cool mountain air that makes him so hungry. I'm sure all the exercise he's been getting helps too. For a snack between meals I've seen him eat a dozen hot, freshly baked biscuits. His breakfast as a rule consists of five huge pancakes, two eggs, eight or nine strips of bacon, and then half an hour later another half a dozen biscuits. The other day there were only four people in camp and I baked two and a half dozen tea biscuits, four different times and they were all gone by three o'clock. The hardest part of baking is keeping enough wood cut so the stove can be kept at an even temperature.

To make biscuits for breakfast meant crawling out of my moderately warm sleeping bag and running to the cook tent to get the fire going and the tent warmed up for the hunters and guides. Some mornings I didn't bother pulling on my ice cold blue jeans before I high tailed it to the cook tent. I waited until they got nice and warm by the fire before I put them on. To keep warm at night I often wore Ted's old brown quilted nylon one piece long johns with a zipper in the seat. When surprised by one of our hunters, an unusually early riser one morning, I must have been quite the sight for there I stood in Ted's long johns with gray work socks pulled up to my knees over top of them and my high top runners on my feet. I wasn't too surprised when later that morning I heard him say to Ted, " now I understand why you two don't have any children." All I can say is this was quite a change from my fashion conscious youth when my hair, clothing and make up had to be perfect before I left the bathroom in the morning.

   The strangest thing happened the other day. Here we were miles from town in a tent when out of nowhere in walks some guy. We were more than a little surprised to say the least. It was pouring rain and the poor guy was soaked through, freezing cold and really hungry. He told us he had been following the telegraph trail and had started out in the Vanderhoof area of central B. C. Said he had been living off of the land, eating whatever fish he could catch and even the odd owl. We fed him, gave him some food to take with him and sent him on his way. When we contacted Atlin on the radio a few days later they said he was now in town.

Chapter 11

Dry Lake Camp

September 17, 1982

Boy, am I ever glad that we brought all the winter clothing that we own into camp with us. It surely gets cold! I've had meat in the Coleman cooler for over a week now and it's still frozen solid. I just set the cooler in the creek and it acts as a giant freezer. If you fill muffin tins with water in the morning when you get up, by the time you get back from the day's hunting you have a good supply of ice cubes for drinks. Imagine doing the laundry and bathing in this ice cold water. It has poured rain every day but three since we arrived in camp. It rains most of the time here as we're sitting in a deep valley surrounded by mountains and the clouds have to drop their moisture in order to get over the mountain.

Our Florida hunters almost froze to death. They couldn't believe anyone would live in this cold, wet, country by choice.

You can surely tell our sleeping bags aren't good ones as I have to use two at once or I'm shivering so badly I can't sleep. I put one inside the other plus wear Ted's long johns. I'm always cold and can't remember the last time I felt warm. We surely take things like running water and heat for granted in the outside world.

   We have a new, two way radio in camp now that the plane dropped off on its last trip in. The one we've been using up until now was an antique and wouldn't pick up much. I'm supposed to monitor the radio for an hour each morning and then another hour each night.

   There's all kinds of fresh grizzly sign around camp now. I hope I never run into one. Our last group of hunters saw five different grizzly's while hunting in the area. There has been a sow and cub hanging around fairly close to camp. The first week we were here I hardly slept at all as I was too busy worrying about bears. Now I sleep with one eye open. I don't really feel that a tent is a lot of protection from a grizzly and If I do run into one, I'll probably just drop dead from fright and won't have to worry about it.

   Little did I know that just one year later in this same camp I would run into one.

   We've had a couple of snowfalls lately and ice forms on the water in the cook tent every night. I usually haul water to the tent from the creek in the evening so it's ready for the next morning. I keep two plastic garbage pails with lids full at all times.

   We have hooked up a small pop-up wood stove in our tent in the last few days. The hunters already had one but we didn't as there is no wood to spare. With this camp sitting right at tree line all firewood has to be hauled in by horse. This is a big chore and a tedious job that takes a lot of extra time and effort.

   You should see me trying to split firewood. What a comedy of errors! As everyone knows I'm the most uncoordinated person in the world so, when I swing the axe I usually miss what I'm aiming at. More than once I've hit my knee with the axe instead of the wood. I can usually find someone to take pity on me and help once they've seen my performance. Oh well as I said before don't mind being the camps entertainment.

Hope this letter finds all well at your end. Please keep writing as we love to hear from you. We feel so isolated out here and love to catch up on the outside worlds news. I will write more later when I have a chance.

Hi again. We've had a busy day today so while I have a few moments to myself I thought I'd fill you in on our news.

Ted, another guide and a hunter shot a grizzly today and are outside of the cook tent right now fleshing out the hide. It's a pretty bear, dark in color with a blonde saddle. They had quite the story to tell upon their arrival back in camp.

A grizzly was spotted close to the spot where the last hunter shot the moose in the lake. Ted went in one direction to keep an eye on the bear as it had disappeared into the brush soon after they spotted it. Meanwhile, the other guide and the hunter split up and went in two different directions. All of a sudden up popped the grizzly right in front of the hunter and heading straight for him at a pretty good clip. The hunter shot at the bear and in all of the excitement hit the bear in the shoulder not doing much to slow him down. Now the bear was good and mad and as he kept up his charge he would run for a short distance then swing around and bite at his shoulder. Mad is an understatement. Ted just happened to be close to the horses at this time and was able to grab a 30-30 rifle out of a scabbard that was strapped to one of the horses sides. He snapped off a quick shot at the bear and wonder of wonders the bear fell over dead instantly. He had hit it in the head with his shot. The shot was nothing but a fluke, we figure the bear must have bent his head down to bite at his stinging shoulder just as Ted pulled the trigger.

We never did let on that the shot wasn't intentional.

For the rest of the season how good a shot Ted was, was the main topic of conversation. Everyone kept saying how lucky the hunter and guide were that Ted was there. We always have a good chuckle over this. Ted is always so calm and cool in an emergency. If everyone had panicked the hunter could have been badly hurt.

Once the bear was dead though the work was just starting. The guide came back to camp to let me know what all the shooting was that I could hear off in the distance and to pick up a camera. While he was in camp, Ted and the hunter got busy and started to prepare the grizzly for transport on the horses. The horses greatly fear bears and to get one to pack a bear was a chore in itself. Once they got a good close up look at the bear, Ted told the hunter that he was almost sure that this wasn't the original bear they had spotted and to keep his eyes open. He thought this bear was lighter in color. After studying the bear they both decided it must have been the angle of light that made it look that way and that it must be the same bear. Sure enough though, just a few moments later, up popped another grizzly making his way towards the gut pile from the last hunters' moose kill. Keeping perfectly still the men watched as the bear went directly to the kill and started to feed. When the other guide returned with the camera he stood guard with a loaded rifle while Ted and the hunter prepared the dead bear for travel in case the feeding bear decided he didn't want them in the vicinity of his dinner. The feeding bear was only three hundred yards from where they were working. When they left to come back to camp, the hungry bear was still there feeding on the kill. Personally I think they're all nuts. Had it been me I would have left both bears where they were and high tailed it straight back to camp.

Guess what I was doing while all these interesting things were going on? As usual I was back in camp baking. Today I baked four dozen bread rolls and some cookies. Three people ate over two dozen cookies for supper. I have only three left out of the thirty I baked. Looks like I'll have to bake again tomorrow.

Must run and help skin and salt the bear hide. Will write more later.

I'm back. I just finished making an enormous pot of caribou stew, baked sixty oatmeal cookies and sixty chocolate chip cookies and some old fashioned raisin muffins. The muffins are all gone already.

Today was washday, the most dreaded day of the week. This afternoon I did a huge wash with the scrub board and a bar of sunlight soap in the ice cold glacial creek. There was so much laundry that I used almost an entire bar of soap. Tonight my hands are chapped bright red and crack open and bleed when I bend my fingers. Ted gets his clothing covered in blood just about every day so there's always lots of laundry to do. Often I do the hunters laundry or they run out of clean clothes. Last night when Ted came into the cook tent to sit by the fire for a few minutes, his pants were covered in bear brains so I made him wash that pair himself today. I have a problem wringing out the laundry as my hands aren't very big and are usually sore. It's much easier for him to do so.

I'm going to go with the men for a few days so I will write more on my return to camp and let you know how things go. Must run, bye for now.

Hi there, I arrived back in camp yesterday and enjoyed the change of scenery. Once back I spent the rest of the day baking as usual. I baked one hundred bread rolls, two batches of muffins and sixty cookies. I guess you can tell what I do with most of my time. It would be so much easier just to go to the store and buy the things we need, but I guess since there is no store that's not an option.

One of our native guides left camp unexpectedly

yesterday. A message came through that his wife was having her baby earlier than expected. What that means to us is that Ted has to guide Doug's hunters as well as his own until they can find another experienced guide to fly into camp. In the next few weeks he's supposed to get his hunters two moose, two caribou, two mountain goat, one grizzly and one black bear. If he succeeds in doing this we'll be here until next spring trying to get them all skinned, fleshed, and salted, and the meat hauled back into camp.

The men just set out to stake out the horses for the night. One of the hunters went with Ted as there's been grizzly hanging around the area where we have been staking out the horses. The grazing is getting poor all over now as the horses have just about everything within reach of camp cropped down pretty close. As a result, we have to keep moving them farther and farther away from the camp at night. Tonight we have them at the far end of the lake in a grassy little meadow. If the bears don't bother them they should get a good feed tonight. It takes an hour or more to stake them out and get back to camp and after a hard day's hunt it's not a chore that anyone particularly wants to do. Being so far from camp means that morning comes an hour earlier, as the horses have to be rounded up and brought back into camp, saddled, breakfast over with and everyone ready to leave by first light.

If a hunter does get an animal during the day's hunt it means that after the horses have been staked out for the night, dinner over with and the hunters are in bed, the guides and cooks have yet to cape out the hides, and get them ready for transport. The meat has to be taken care of, so the blow fly's don't ruin it by laying eggs all over it. I'm getting really good at turning the ears and lips, a time consuming job that everyone hates. I try to help out where ever I can or poor Ted would never get to bed at night.

It was two degrees below freezing this morning.

I keep shoving Ted out of bed at night to put wood in the stove. He's really a good sport about it as I guess he's probably as cold as I am and is glad for the heat.

The moose are starting to rutt now. One of the pilots saw two good size bulls fighting close to our camp as he was flying over the other day.

There are lots of wild blueberries and mossberries around right now but I have no intentions of picking any as where there are berries there are bears. I'd rather go without.

I'm sure our new hunters from New York didn't have any idea what this country would be like when they came. Now they're trying to figure out what they got themselves into. Both of them are in their late forty's and in poor shape. They weigh between two hundred and two seventy five each. Our poor tired horses can hardly carry them. They don't want to do any walking at all and climbing is out of the question. Yesterday, Ted tried to get them into the high country where the caribou are but they wanted Ted to go by himself and take a look around. Then if he saw anything worthwhile, they wanted him to come and get them. They thought they would be able to just sit on a horse and have the horse climb the mountain with them on its back. Surprise, that's not the way it works! Today they came back to camp for an afternoon nap between two and five. Both of them have goat tags but we told them to think twice before trying to go after goat as they would never make it. We've had a good time and a lot of laughs with them. At least they can see the humor in the situation and are having a great time despite all the draw backs.

It's really windy and the wind keeps lifting the chimney out of the stove in the cook tent. When this happens, there are sparks flying everywhere. The first time this happened I was alone in camp in the dark and almost had heart failure until I figured out what was going on. We get lots of wind in this valley. It showered rain a while ago, but is clear again now. When the sky's clear at night it sure gets cold up here.

I heard on the radio phone earlier tonight that someone in Whitehorse was mauled by a grizzly just outside of town the other day. Apparently the guy had shot a moose and went back into town to get help getting the moose out. He was so excited at having actually gotten the moose he left his rifle in town and then headed back out to bring the meat in. As he started to cape out the moose a grizzly jumped him from behind. Luckily his help arrived in the nick of time and was able to scare the bear off. Lucky guy! When they got him to the hospital, they were surprised to see that he was okay. I love hearing stories like this especially when I'm alone in camp.

I made Bannoch (fried bread) for breakfast this a.m. and it was a big hit. Most of our American hunters have never heard of it but really like it. Sometimes I throw a few wild berries in it or make mossberry syrup to pour over it. Mom, I find that your recipe from Kitiimat Indian Village is by far the best one I've come across.

Right now is the time I should be monitoring the radio but I feel spooky tonight and am too scared to go to the radio tent alone in the dark so, it's not getting done. I don't think I'll ever get used to being not only the only person within miles but alone in the dark on a mountain. As the radio tent is on the other side of the river and I can't find the flashlight I'm staying right here.

I learned early on that if one walks in the dark carrying a lantern they will be blinded by the light. I learned this lesson well one night when Ted and the hunters played a trick on me. I should have been suspicious when Ted handed me the lantern and offered to carry my shot gun for me. As we set off down the trail suddenly there was a big commotion in the bushes a short distance away. I was in the process of fading dead away when I finally figured out that everyone was having a good laugh at my actions as I scrambled for my shot gun. The guys had staked the horses out close to the trail as they were late getting into camp and had decided not to tell me so they could see what my reaction would be. I thought it was a dirty trick but they all thought I was hysterically funny. Oh well, another good laugh was had by all but me.

The following morning when I did monitor the radio we learned that we would be leaving this camp in a couple of days. Before we left though the camp had to be closed up tight as no one else would be in here for the rest of the season. Leftover food like flour, sugar, beans etc. were stored in plastic bags and then sealed in plastic garbage pails with tight fitting lids. This would protect things from the animals. This system seemed to work as good or better than the well known tree cache.

Finally with everything closed up we were ready to go. When the Beaver did arrive the water level in the lake was so low the plane could only get off of the lake carrying one person at a time. It was decided that I would be the first person to be flown out and that I would be dropped off at Paddy Lake Camp while the plane returned to Dry Lake to get another person. Together we would then head back into Atlin. I would stay in town for a couple of days then fly into another camp to help cook for a few days. Ted and the Dry Lake hunters, plus the editor of Peterson's hunting magazine, would hunt their way across country bringing the entire pack string of horses with them. I would meet them at Paddy Lake Camp in a week or so as I would fly back into that camp on the plane that was scheduled to fly the hunters out. Our next hunters would fly in with me.

Thanks to Ted's great sense of dirrection the guys did pretty well at keeping the schedule on their cross country trip and were only an hour late. There was a mad rush sorting gear and trophies, quick good-byes were said, addresses exchanged, and in no time at all the plane was lifting off of the lake and slowly disappearing out of sight.

Chapter 12

Paddy Lake Camp

September 22, 1982
Dear Mom and Dad,
    As you can see I'm in a different camp since I last wrote to you. Paddy Lake is a pretty spot, a lot lower in altitude than Dry Lake was. We are only at about three thousand feet here. It's a nice change and is quite a bit warmer than higher up.
    This camp is located on the historic Telegraph Trail and is nestled in a buck brush covered meadow on the edge of a crystal clear lake. Looking across the lake we see heavily timbered mountain sides, and higher up above the tree line, lots of bare hill sides. To our right we see rugged snow capped mountains and to our left there is a large grass filled meadow at the lake's end. This is where we usually stake out the horses at night. The horses are happy here as they once again have lots of good food. Behind the camp the timbered mountain sides hide many small lakes and swamps that make for good moose hunting. In the high country behind the camp are herds of caribou and picturesque postcard like caribou camp, where we stay when we are hunting caribou.
    Paddy Lake itself is loaded with fresh water shrimp and is an excellent fishing lake that pro-

duces lots of nice Lake trout and large Northern Pike. The moose are in full rutt now. There are lots of them around this area. You never know where you'll run into one. We're having a bit of a problem keeping them away from our horses at the moment. I guess the moose figure they've found paradise when they come across so many horses in one spot all conveniently tied to trees just waiting for them. I've come to the conclusion that the moose don't care if they're horses but the horses surely do.

The other night we had a two year old bull moose walk up and touch noses with our largest horse while the horse was staked out in the meadow. We were just sitting down to relax when we heard a lot of commotion coming from the horses. We ran outside to see what was happening and quite a sight greeted us. The little two year old bull moose had decided that he was in love with Danny, one of the horses. The fact that the horse was quite a bit larger than himself didn't seem to bother him at all. As he walked up to touch noses Ted ran and grabbed our camera. We should have some interesting and unusual pictures.

We had a grizzly bawling in the meadow where the horses are staked out the other night. He bawled all night long. It sounded like a young one that the sow had just kicked out and it wanted its mom. The horses were pretty spooked all the next day.

There have been two grizzly attacks in the Dry Lake area lately. The editor of a well known hunting magazine, and two guides shot a grizzly that was feeding on a caribou kill. When they walked up to look at the bear and started to get it ready for transport, a sow grizzly with two cubs charged them trying to claim the bear kill. They finally drove the bears away with gunfire. Later on during the same hunt, the hunter shot a nice goat that slid down a chute on the side of the mountain after he was shot. The two guides went down the chute after the goat leaving their rifles up top. Stretching out to relax, the hunter watched as the guides headed towards the goat when suddenly he caught movement out of the corner of his eye. There was a large grizzly bear heading for the same goat as the men. When eventually the bear and the guides met in the middle, they both turned and took off in opposite directions. The hunter watched as the bear suddenly skidded to a stop and turning ran back towards the goat and the men. By this time the hunter was shooting down the mountainside at a distance of about 800 yards, trying to scare the bear away and give the men time to make good their escape. Running out of bullets he grabbed one of the guide's 30-30 rifles and ran back towards the men shooting downhill to keep the bear at bay while the guides made good their escape leaving the goat to the hungry bear. They figure what happened was that when they shot the goat and it fell down the chute, it must have slid right past the bear who decided that it was dinner. They were lucky that no one was hurt! In this area it got so bad that if anyone shot a rifle the bears came running, just a though the shot was a dinner bell.

There were a lot of grizzly around Dry Lake when we were there. Ted saw twenty different grizzly in that area. He saw eight at one time on one hillside. I was kind of glad to leave that area to the bears. In that area the bears were pretty thin where as in other areas this year they are nice and fat and not so hungry.

Paddy Lake Camp is an interesting camp and has quite a history. There are two old cabins here, the cook shack that Ted and I also sleep in and another one that the hunters use to sleep in. The cook shack has two narrow bunks made out of old boards that are attached to the wall. The cabin itself was built in the late 1880's and was initially used as a line shack when the historic Telegraph Trail was being pushed through this remote area. The cabin is quite the sight made partially of rotting logs and partially of old boards with a falling down entrance porch attached to one end. Across the cabin's front, are a few broken windows that have been mended with plastic over the years. Sometime in the past, someone has tacked up old newspaper tintypes over the spots where the walls have rotted through. The door is roughly five feet high. To reach it one must first pass through a falling down entrance porch with a wooden board floor that is rotted through in places exposing the dirt below. The cabin's inner walls are covered in bits and pieces of paper and cardboard to help keep out the drafts. The inner floors are in different stages of rot and there are holes through to the dirt in some areas, in others the floor has totally caved in leaving the damp earth below exposed. Sometime in the distant past, someone has dragged in part of an old rusty tin pop-up stove that acts as our only means of heat and also doubles as a cook stove.

The walls inside the cabin are a real study as over the last hundred years they have been used as a message post. They tell the story of births, deaths, of where people were headed and why and when people would pass through again on their return trip. One message was in the late eighteen hundreds and told of the death of the chief and named the New Chief. Another told of the death of someone by a bear.

Mike Oros, who called himself Rev. Sheslea Free Mike, and who in the past had murdered a local trapper and in the future would murderer an R.C.M.P. officer, used this cabin often. His psychotic ramblings were all over the walls. The young R.C.M.P. officer Mike would shoot, was due to get married the next day. Mike would soon be the target of a full scale search and shoot out with the R.C.M.P., the search included dogs, helicopters, float planes and snow shoes. Just sitting and reading the cabin's walls was an education in itself.

This cabin would be our new home for the next while and I for one was glad to have four walls around me once again. The cabin felt like a palace to me.

One hundred yards from this cabin stands another one roughly the same age but in a bit better state of repair. It's used by a trapper as a trap cabin in the winters. We didn't know it but in the future we would also spend a winter living in this cabin while we trapped this area with our dear friend George.

The lake is teaming with fresh water shrimp and the water must be strained before we can use it. The fishing is excellent here partly due to the fact that the fish eat the shrimp.

We heard on the radio today that our boss and his wife got a nice caribou on their hunt. While they were skinning it out and getting it ready for transport, a good size grizzly tried to take it away from them. They were finally able to scare the bear off with gun fire but I guess it was a pretty close call. While they were heading down the mountain with the caribou horns, it got dark so they decided to set up a camp for the night. While scouting around for firewood with a flashlight they saw a glimpse of white and decided to investigate. What they found was an enormous moose rack. It looked like the moose had probably died of natural causes earlier in the year. Because the rack was so big they decided to bring it out with them. I turned out to be the third largest Canadian pick up rack ever recorded the rack measuring sixty seven and one half inches. A big moose!

Ted had a real winner to guide on our last hunt. None of the other guides would guide him and all threatened to quit if they had to, so Ted inherited him. Lucky Ted! He was after a moose but nothing pleased him and he just about drove everyone in camp nuts. All he wanted to do was take pictures with his new video camera. Ted showed him ten nice bull moose in one afternoon and he was upset that there weren't enough to choose from. Every time Ted found him a moose he would make Ted get off of his horse and pretend to stalk the thing while he took pictures. Ted showed him two exceptionally nice moose while he was in camp but he never did shoot one. We figure the one moose Ted showed him was well over a sixty inch spread and the other one would have been close to sixty. Both were big moose in any one's book! When Ted spotted the largest moose, the moose was quite a distance away from them but was still in shooting range. By the time the guy finished playing with his camera, the moose was out of range. Ted got his revenge though, he worked the guy so hard that Ted was ready to drop. Big revenge!

    This hunter was in camp for a week and during the week almost succeeded in getting himself run over by an angry bull moose. He was so busy taking pictures that he didn't realize that the moose was charging him. I almost had heart failure before Ted was able to scare off the moose by shooting his gun in the air above it's head. We were all glad to see him finally leave camp as he pulled some mighty stupid stunts while here. I got my revenge though as I pulled a dirty trick on him. He was about to drive me nuts as he was such a picky eater and used to do things like order his breakfast in bed in his cabin, not that he ever got it in bed. One day I sat and thought about what I could do to get him back for all the irritating things he was doing. I knew he liked puddings for dessert at night so one night I made him pistachio pudding only I didn't strain the fresh water shrimp out of the water I used. He loved the pudding and thought the crunchy shrimp were extra nuts.

Chapter 13

Moose Calling

One of the hunters we had in our camp lately shot a moose with a fifty-four inch rack not too far from the cook shack. Everyone was out hunting one day except me and one hunter who had already shot a moose. He had decided to hang around camp and relax while the others went hunting. He was sleeping in his cabin when I suddenly heard a moose grunting and carrying on high on the mountain across the lake from the cook shack. Deciding to have some fun, I woke the hunter and told him to come with me. When we arrived at the lake's edge, I started to call the moose in by grunting and splashing in the water. Down the mountain he came, thrashing the bushes, grunting and carrying on. Upon reaching a small clearing across from us, about two-hundred and seventy-five yards away, he stopped and stood still while we got a good look at him. He was quite the sight to see. There stood this majestic animal, dirt and moss and tree branches hanging from his horns, snorting and stomping his feet and pawing at the ground around him. About that time the hunter decided he liked this moose better than the one he had already shot and I almost had to tie him up to keep him from shooting it. We had a lot of fun watching it and I was able to keep the bull there for about two hours by grunting and calling to it. Several times he started across the lake towards us but luckily turned and returned to his own side. When the hunters finally returned to camp empty handed they shot him. It was an experience of a life time! I had been practicing my moose call but never really thought a moose would come to it. Guess that goes to show that moose aren't fussy when they are in rutt.

I had a dandy scare the other day. Everyone was away from camp hunting except for myself and Brian a young wrangler about seventeen years old. Being from Nevada he hadn't spent much time in the bush but was learning his job as he went along. What a brave little soul he turned out to be! I was sitting outside the cook shack soaking up the sunshine and the beauty and peacefulness of the area, when all of a sudden I spotted a huge grizzly bear swimming down the center of the lake heading straight for our camp. As I didn't have a gun in this camp and Brian only had a 30-30 rifle with one shell left, we were in big trouble. We were both running in circles trying to figure out what to do when Brian said, "Bonnie, you get up on the cabin roof and I'll stay here and do my best with what I've got." About this time we both turned to see where the bear was and were both surprised to see that it wasn't a grizzly at all, only a big old cross fox with his tail streaming out behind him in the water. The way his tail and back were sticking out of the water made him look just like a big old grizzly to us. I have never forgotten this brave young wrangler and how he was going to protect me with only one shell in his 30-30 rifle. This country has a lot of cross foxes. They are a cross between a red fox and a silver fox. They have a distinct dark colored cross that runs down the center of their back and across the front legs.

One night while we were sleeping in the cook shack and everything was nice and peaceful, the horses decided they wanted the oats that were stored in the falling down porch attached to the front of our cabin. Instead of staking out all of the horses this particular night we had some hobbled and left the most trustworthy ones loose. Big mistake! As the evening progressed, we had to keep chasing them out of the porch and would no sooner get back to sleep when the noise of their hooves on the rotting board floor would wake us all over again. Finally, fed up, Ted signaled for me to be quiet and he crept silently over towards the door leading to the outside porch. The next thing I knew, He threw open the door and roared like a bear at the horses. I thought the entire cabin was going to fall down on top of me as there was a mad scramble for the door. We could hear the loose horses taking off at a gallop in every direction and the hobbled horses were so scared they were keeping up with them with no problem at all. Peace finally reigned and we slept peacefully the rest of the night. The next day we spent over half the day trying to locate the spooked horses before anyone could go hunting. It's amazing how fast and how far a hobbled horse can go.

Another time while hunting out of this camp, Ted's hunter shot a nice bull moose from the edge of the lake right below the cook shack. The problem was that the moose was on the other side of the lake and we didn't have a boat to go and get it. The river between us and the moose had high water at this time of year, so, reaching the moose turned out to be quite a chore.

As there was no rope to be found, the men built a raft by tying old rotting boards together with string. On they hopped and using another board as a paddle, paddled across the lake. Once there, the moose had to be skinned and the meat taken care of. We hung the quarters of meat in a tree close to shore so that the float plane could taxi up to it to get it on its next trip into camp. Next we had to figure out a way to get the heavy moose head and horns plus two people back to camp. The head had to be skinned out properly and the hide taken care of so it wouldn't spoil. As they worked the wind picked up and the water got a pretty good chop on it. Knowing both men plus the moose head could never cross on this raft it was decided that Ted would go on the raft with the moose head and that the hunter would walk to the far end of the lake and cross at the swollen river. I ran for my camera and zoom lens when I saw Ted standing on the little raft that was held together with string.

Holding his jacket wide open he was using it as a sail while the wind blew the raft down the lake towards the cabin.

One of our hunters got a record book goat this week. It was shot on the mountain we can see to the right of camp. It's really a nice goat. They are beautiful with their full pantaloons. From a distance they look so snowy white and clean but up close one can see they are coated in dust and mud.

It won't be long now until we'll be heading out of camp for the winter. I know we'll miss being in the bush and we'll miss all of the new friends we've made this season. We have both enjoyed our time in the mountains and have learned that the excitement of the hunt is most addictive. We are already looking forward to next year.

I must close now as I have to start closing up the camp today. I can hardly wait to show you all of the pictures we've been taking. Then you'll be able to see just how beautiful this country is and why we love it so much. The plane is due in to get us in the next couple of days.

Chapter 14

Home Again

Hi there,
　　Well here we are back in Atlin again. We have decided to stay in town and look after the lodge for the winter while the owners go back to the states. The lodge is huge, thirty five hundred square feet compared to the less than four hundred of our cabin. We thought it would be nice to have running water and electricity for a change. I know we'll enjoy the telephone too.
　　I'll keep in touch and who knows you might even get a surprise phone call one of these days.
　　It surely feels good to have a real bed after all the months we spent in hunting camp living in tents.

　　The winter turned out to be a quiet one for us and in the spring we moved back into our cabin. After staying in town for the winter we enjoyed the stillness and solitude of the cabin's surroundings.
　　Ted was able to get lots of work on the new Atlin Airport in 1983, so much so that we didn't go guiding at all the next fall. Besides working on the airport, Ted took a job helping to build a huge cabin at a remote wilderness camp on the Taku River.

We had finally heard back from the government and had started to build our log house on our own land. Building our log home kept us more than busy. George and Goldy had also started to build a beautiful home close to where we were building.

Our home is a lot bigger than the cabin and we are enjoying all of the room. We have two bedrooms, one up and one down, a big kitchen, living room, storage loft and walk in cold room that's attached to the kitchen. One sure enjoys what one works so hard to get. We are located close to Atlin Lake and about two and a half miles from the town. Just a nice walking distance.

Later that year we were fortunate enough to be able to afford to take a trip back east to Ontario for Christmas. Although we enjoyed surprising Ted's family, we found city life a lot different than we had grown used to and could hardly wait to return home to the peace and quiet of living in the bush.

While we were visiting Ted's brother and his family, our dear friend George phoned us and asked us if we wanted to help him work a trap line for the winter as he'd been lucky enough to find one to lease from a friend. Good trap lines were in great demand. Few were for rent and almost none were for sale. Naturally we jumped at the chance to rent this one. Here began another of our great adventures.

January 11, 1984
Dear mom and dad,
Well, here I am back at Paddy Lake cabin and no one is more surprised than I am. This is the last place I thought I'd ever be at this time of year. It's winter as you know although living in Vancouver it's sometimes hard to tell. This time we're here trapping not hunting. I'll try and fill you in on my surroundings.

I really wonder what I'm doing here when I look around. Oh well, at least I'm not sitting home alone although sometimes I'm not too sure what the lesser of the two evils is. I'm not complaining as there's not much sense doing so, I just have to look around myself and laugh for if I started to cry I'm sure I would never quit. No really it's not all that bad, but then I've only been here two days. Ask me again what I think at the end of March. We are in the cabin that the hunters stayed in when we last hunted out of this camp.

   We had a great trip from town to our first trap cabin on Monday. It's located about forty miles from town but, if the weather is good, one can usually drive a couple miles of it. We traveled by snowmobile through some beautiful, rugged country. It was crisp and sunny when we left town and the snow was sparkling like diamonds all around us. The combination of blue shadows, sparkling white snow and clear blue sky and sunshine was intoxicating. I enjoyed this part of our trip tremendously, although novice that I am on a snowmobile, I had a few good scares and just about drove the men crazy with some of my antics. On some of the steep side hills I would slide off of my machine and bog down in the deep snow. This was always a big hit and helped to endear me to the men as when this happened it meant that either one or both of them would have to stop, struggle back through the thigh high snow carrying a heavy shovel and dig me out. Then they would have to make their way back to their own machines, start them and get on their way again. Usually about this time, someone would turn around to see how I was doing, only to find that once again I wasn't behind them. Then the entire process would begin again. I found that as I sat and waited for help, for some reason I would find myself silently praying that it would be George that came to my rescue. George had far more patience with me than Ted at the moment. By the time we had covered the first twenty miles of trails through deep snow, across open creeks, along steep hill sides and through narrow brush trails where willows abounded and had a way of reaching out to slap one in the face when least expected, I was a real pro and could go through almost anything.

It didn't take me long to learn that the first thing I needed to do as my machine buried itself in the deep snow was to concentrate on making sure that at least one of my arms or legs ended up sticking out of the snow so the men could find me. By the end of trapping season we would each put roughly fifteen hundred miles on our snowmobiles.

Chapter 15

Trapping

The first trap cabin, a ten foot by twelve foot log structure, was extremely warm. Inside it had two single size plywood bunk beds, a two foot by two foot table made of boards, a tiny cupboard, and a huge fifty-five gallon drum that had been made into a wood stove. As the stove was way too large for the tiny cabin, we had to keep the cabins door open at all times. Ted slept on the floor, George got the bottom bunk, and I got the top bunk that no one else wanted because of the heat. At night I'd lie in my bunk and look outside at the trees and the snow around the cabin through the open doorway as I drifted off to sleep.

Temperatures would drop as low as -40 degrees Fahrenheit while we stayed in this cabin and not once did we close the door. If I turned my head while I lay on my bunk, I could enjoy the scenery that was visible through the eaves where the insulation had been removed in an effort to cool the cabin down and let the air circulate. It was surely hot in the top bunk. Now I know why no one else wanted it. The stove usually burned itself out around 5 a.m. and about that time George and I would throw anything we could reach at Ted to wake him so he could slither across the floor in his sleeping bag and get the fire going again. We all appreciated our sleeping bags and long johns then.

We stayed in this cabin for a couple of nights while the men set traps and checked the ones that they had already set. We found they had gotten lucky and had caught six Martin, also called Sable. They were bringing about seventy-five dollars each at the time.

Early one morning with breakfast finished and the cabin closed up, we once again set off by snowmobile this time for Paddy Lake cabin twenty miles away.

If all had gone as planned we should have arrived at the cabin in the early afternoon, but the weather had turned so mild that we had nothing but trouble with the snowmobiles the entire way.

```
Hello again,
```
The trails the men had made on a previous trip were all really soft and the machines kept bogging down and getting stuck in the heavy wet snow. Ted was pulling a heavy sled loaded with supplies that kept bogging down on him and getting his snowmobile stuck. As he had all the traps, extra gas and supplies on the sled, there was nothing we could do but keep on going a bit at a time. We ended up having to pull the heavy sled up the steeper side hills by hand. We did this by two people pulling and the other person pushing. A couple of times we still just about didn't make it. On top of this problem we had an even bigger one, we had five different lakes to cross.

With the weather being so mild we got stuck in the over flow on every single lake. Over flow is caused by the heavy snow on top of the ice making the ice sink. When the ice sinks, water gets on top of the ice and under the snow. It is just about impossible to spot a stretch of over flow before it's too late and your already stuck. The over flow can get quite deep. Many times we've been stuck in a couple of feet of water. When this happens we have to stop every couple of hundred yards and dig out all three machines. On one lake George made it across okay, but Ted's machine and mine both went through the overflow and both were stuck. As we couldn't budge either of them without George's help, he parked his machine and walked back across the lake to help dig us out, going through the overflow with every step. He ended up freezing one foot a little before he was able to get back to his snowmobile and his dry clothes. Finally, all of us arrived on the far side of the overflow. To do this Ted had the job of breaking a new trail around the lake on foot. He then took my snowmobile and followed his trail. Then he walked back across the lake in water up to his knees to get his own machine. Great for everyone but me as all this left me on the wrong side of the lake without a machine. So, I had no choice but to walk across the overflow and let me tell you I wasn't thrilled with that idea. I don't know how but up until this time I had managed to keep my feet dry and as we still had a long way to go to the cabin I really would have liked to keep them dry. Finally, with no other choice, I set off to walk across. I decided that if Jesus could walk on water so could I and praying all the way I kept on going never breaking through the ice once. Ted and George kept yelling directions to me on where I should walk and I kept yelling back for them to be quiet as I was walking on water by faith alone and was doing just fine without their help. We all had a good laugh over this.

Finally with three machines and all three people safely on the far side of the lake, we were on our way once again. We were lucky and only got stuck in overflow about four more times before we rounded the bend and the cabin came into view. I made it all the way with dry feet. Don't ask me how as everyone else was soaked.

Boy, did the cabin ever look good by the time we got here until I opened the door. After twenty miles of over flow and poor trails, and after nine hours on a snowmobile in the freezing cold, I thought I'd cry when I saw the mess that the cabin was in. It does grow on one though and after two days of cleaning and two nights of sleep it doesn't look nearly as bad as it had. It's actually quite comfortable and homey. This cabin was built around the turn of the century and consists of one room roughly twelve feet by twelve feet. The walls are lined with cardboard for warmth and it has a board floor, tin roof, and two wooden bunks the top one being double in size. It has a tin Yukon stove with a badly rusted oven that is not usable, and also has a tin pop-up stove for heat. Off to one side of the room stands a large wooden cupboard. We use the top of the cupboard for a table. We have one halfway decent chair, one with no back, and we use a stump for the third. The cupboard doubles as a cache when everyone's away from camp as we can store anything that we don't want the animals getting into inside of it. Actually we have no complaints and are quite comfortable.

We were lucky and got eight more Martin in our traps the other day on our way here from the other cabin. The men worked until midnight last night stretching and skinning them. I had them on the floor thawing under the Yukon stove all day yesterday and boy do they ever stink! Now the carcasses are gone and I just have the furs all over. Am I ever thankful for my can of Raid!

The doorway into the cabin, like most old cabins, is only about five feet high. I have two large goose eggs on my forehead so far. This morning I hung fluorescent orange surveyors tape all over the top door sill in hopes that this will remind all of us to duck.

The out house here is really unique. It consists of a log frame with faded blue canvas draped around it. It's poised high on the hill behind the cabin and over looks the whole lake and surrounding area. I guess I shouldn't complain as the out house at the other cabin was just a hole in the ground and one had to lean back over the hole hanging on to some willows to keep from falling in. In cold weather one had to be especially careful that the willows didn't snap or you were in deep trouble.

This morning I washed my hair in the dishpan, and then did my laundry in it. I washed some wool socks for the men and some of their long johns. They are now hanging on nails all over the cabin and are dripping all over the floor. As my hands are pretty small I couldn't wring all the water out of the wool socks and they are now three feet long and two inches wide. The men will be impressed with this I'm sure. I bet they won't complain too loudly though as I know they won't want to end up doing their own laundry.

We stamped out an airstrip in the snow on the lake in front of the cabin the other day. The Beaver delivered two barrels of gas and some groceries to us. We had made arrangements for this delivery the last time we were in town. It cost us $350 for the flight so the gas ended up costing us roughly six dollars per gallon by the time it got here. I can see already that this trapping is a rich man's hobby not a poor man's living.

I have a squirrel for company when the men are away in the daytime. He lives between the cardboard and the tin roof. Silly little thing keeps chewing the cardboard into little pieces and it really makes a big mess. Ted set a trap for him this morning.

When we first arrived at this cabin we brought with us a five gallon pail of three year old rotten fish to use as trap bait. The smell has gotten into everything including our clothing and sleeping bags. Washing doesn't help the odor in the least, so, it's something that all of us have gotten used to and don't notice much anymore. Can you imagine what we must smell like to an outsider! On top of this pleasant fish odor, George has skunk scent all over his snowmobile suit from wiping his hands on it when he's setting the traps. I have no idea why he thinks the suit has to hang by the head of our beds at night.

For some unexplained reason skunk scent seems to attract the animals to the traps. Maybe it's because there are no skunks in this country and the animals are curious as to what the smell is. We've seen the tracks of moose that have walked a long way out of their way to smell a trap that had skunk scent on it.

The temperature is plus twenty and inside the cabin it's at least ninety. I have to keep wood in the stove all the time as I do all of the cooking on top of it. It stays quite warm in here, most nights we don't have to cover up until morning.

Yesterday while the men were away I dug two deep holes in the snow beside the cabin and buried two barrels of food in the snow to help keep it frozen.

There are caribou on most of the smaller lakes now as the snow in the high country is deep making it hard for them to find food.

This is an unusually warm winter and it's been hard on the trappers. It's not only just about impossible to get around, the fur prices are way down as the furs are rubbed already. The furs are never as good when it's warm as they are when it's cold out.

We had a Weasel, Ermine in their white winter stage, running around the cabin the other night while we were trying to sleep. He was into everything, even running around on the beds while we were in them. I guess it goes without saying that I wasn't exactly thrilled at the thought that as soon as I closed my eyes a Weasel was going to jump out of the ceiling and land on me. I was having a fit much to the amusement of the men. Since the men couldn't get to sleep with all of the noise I was making and all of my actions as I tried to avoid having this little creature jump on me in the dark, they finally gave in and set a trap and caught the thing around one thirty a.m. Let me tell you a weasel stinks worse than a skunk when it lets it's scent glands go!

Time to say good bye again as the men are due in soon and they are always starving from all the fresh air and exercise that they get. I'd like to be able to go out with them more than I do but with the price of gas being so high it's not a good idea for me to go. I do enjoy myself when I do get the chance to go and usually end up taking lots of pictures of all of the goings on.

I have no idea when we'll be back in town so I'll just keep adding to this until I get a chance to mail it.

Hi, I'm back again,

It's snowing like mad out today. The men left early this morning, before breakfast, to check their traps. They usually arrive back at the cabin cold, wet through, and hungry just as it's getting dark. We are in snow country in this camp. Hopefully we won't get too much as it's hard to keep the trails open when there's a lot of fresh snow. This area usually has five of six feet but we have only three or four right now.

Tomorrow is the big day when we retrace the twenty mile trip through the overflow to check the traps at the small cabin. We'll stay one night then head back here early the next morning. Actually, the men took a ride over to the trail today to check it out and both said it's in pretty good shape. I'll let you know when we get back just how good.

There was a cow and calf caribou on the lake today. Such a beautiful sight. My squirrel is still in the roof but hopefully will be in the trap soon. He is so destructive.

Guess I better pack for our little trip now so I'll keep in touch as soon as we return.

Well, here I am again still alive and kicking. We made it back from the other cabin but don't ask me how.

On Monday when we left here the weather was beautiful, a bit warm but not too bad overall. We had a good trip and stayed at the small cabin two nights. While at the cabin we checked and reset all the traps we had set in that area. We caught eleven Martin and one Coyote. On our way back to this cabin we did everything but swim.

It was too warm for the snowmobiles and everything was melting, plus, the wind had blown all of our trails in. In some spots we couldn't even find our trails and as if this wasn't bad enough, it even rained on us part way back. Today it's colder again so the men are out checking the traps at this end. Tomorrow we have to make another trip to the other cabin as all the traps we set there will be frozen over from the freezing rain. Best close and try and get a good nights sleep as it's a physically draining trip to the other cabin. Will keep in touch. Must run. Bye for now.

The trip turned out to be a trying experience as the trail was worse than we'd ever seen it. There was a lot of deep over flow on all the lakes. In one spot we actually had to build a road across the lake by using a shovel and putting snow in the water then stomping it down with our feet. Then we added more snow and more tromping, then more snow over and over until we reached the far side of the lake. We then held our breath while the snowmobiles were brought across our ice bridge. The sleds had to be pushed and pulled by hand. To top things off when we finally did reach the cabin in the dark, we were wet and exhausted. After we got the fire going, both men sat with hungry faces waiting for their supper. Naturally they sat and watched me do the dishes, too.

Hello from Paddy Lake cabin. It's twenty degrees today and raining. I have moose meat cooking on top of the stove making the inside of the cabin at least ninety. Hopefully it will taste good and be worth all the heat.

Finally we got rid of the pesky squirrel. It was cute but chewed everything it could get a hold of and made an awful mess. When I was cooking breakfast this morning, he was sitting on the window sill keeping an eye on what I was up to.

I did the laundry this morning, thought you might be interested in knowing that the long skinny socks weren't much of a hit last time.

The trapping hasn't been great for the last while as we've only gotten three martin in the last three days. We're starting to see a lot more lynx, fox, and wolverine tracks but like they say, " tracks make poor soup."

It's been foggy on the mountains lately and today I can't see the sun at all. The overflow causes a lot of ice fog.

Must close but will write more later. Hard to imagine it's the end of January already.

Chapter 16

Snow Shoeing

January 30, 1984

We planned on heading out early on the twenty-ninth to start snow shoeing our way towards the Nakina River. We were just getting ready to go out of the door, when out of nowhere came three men and three dog sleds. They were in training for the big Iditarod dog sled race in Alaska. Their arrival meant I had to start cooking breakfast all over again. Bruce Johnson and his friend, Larry (Cowboy) Smith, had spent the previous night camped on the trail about four miles from our cabin and were cold, hungry, and thankful for hot coffee when they finally got here. One of the sled dogs had wandered off the side of the trail the night before and had stepped in one of our traps but was okay It was quite a sight to see three dog teams with loaded sleds and all the dogs decked out in leather booties to protect their feet. We took some good pictures of them with the trap cabin in the background.

Bruce had a message for me that my Grandfather had passed away a few days earlier. This was a sad time for me as my Grandpa was very special to me. It was hard not being able to say good bye to him as I loved him dearly. He was my special person and I was his.

Bruce, a Yukon Quest champion, and veteran of the Iditarod trail sled dog race, trained his dogs in all types of weather. On November twenty-fourth 1993, the bodies of Bruce and his dogs were recovered from the bottom of little Atlin Lake by the R.C.M.P. divers. Bruce and his dogs went through the ice and drowned while he was training for a race. He was one of the Yukon's top dog mushers and will be missed by all. He was someone most of the other mushers tried to pattern themselves after.

After the dishes were finished once again and everyone had caught up with the latest gossip, the men and dogs were on their way back towards town and we were on ours towards the Nakina River about fifteen miles away. If we thought we were in snow country at the cabin, boy were we in for a surprise as the closer we got to the river the more snow there was.

Heading towards Rainbow Lake where one of our hunting camps is located, we snowshoed almost the entire day away before we realized that the trail we had just made was too steep for the snowmobiles and we would have to try and reach the river again the next day heading in a different direction.

There was over four feet of snow in the valleys we were snowshoeing through and it was a real chore trying to stay on top of it as it hadn't settled yet from the last snowfall. I found snowshoeing to be hard work and found it took a lot of patience and skill going up and down the steep hills. George had a pair of nice new Bear paw snowshoes and Ted had a good pair too. Both of the men enjoyed the invigorating walks in the sparkling white snow and sunshine as we broke trail day after day. I enjoyed being outside in the fresh air but as I had two mismatched snowshoes tied on my feet with an old rubber inner tube and sometimes with string I found every step hard work. At the end of the day every bone in my body would be sore and the men couldn't figure out why I was so tired and they weren't. I dreaded going up hill as without fail my bindings of rubber would let go at a critical moment and I'd find myself having to wade through the chest high snow the rest of the way to the top. Going down hill was just as bad as the pressure of my feet against the bindings would cause them to break and without fail I would go flying onto my back in the deep snow.

Yesterday, the three of us set out at daybreak on our snowshoes, and tried to follow the old Telegraph Trail towards the Nakina River. It turned out to be fairly good walking and hopefully should be good snowmobiling. The snow in this area is deep so we'll have to be especially careful not to go off of the edges of the trail or we'll sink out of sight in the powdery snow. When this happens it's no fun getting the machines back onto the trail, especially for me. Lots of times I find myself pinned under the snowmobile sometimes almost totally buried in snow, alone, and unable to move the machine off of me. The only thing that keeps me from panicking is that I know, sooner or later someone will miss me and will return to try and find me. This thought really doesn't help much when I'm lying in the overflow getting soaking wet as the water under the snow seeps through my clothes. It's surprising what a person can do for one's self when there's no choice and no one else around to help.

Today the men are out checking traps so tomorrow we'll head out on the snow shoes again. Today I'm giving my weary muscles a much needed rest. We have about ten miles of trail yet to break before we'll be able to use the machines. We got a nice cross fox the other day. They are bringing about two hundred and fifty dollars right now. We were surprised to see that the one we just got was already starting to breed and that the fur was rubbed off in some places.

Ted and George have a new gizmo called a tail puller and were anxious to try it on this fox. It's supposed to simplify the skinning of the fox. George's face was a real study when while trying it out he pulled the tail right off the fox.

We have another Weasel in the cabin. He comes out mostly at night when all is quiet.

I just gave the cabin a good cleaning, It took all of about five minutes. I also put a huge pot of bear stew on the stove to simmer for the day so it'll be tender tonight. I must put a pot of water on now so I can wash my hair later. This morning there were three gorgeous sun dogs around the sun. It's supposed to mean cold weather on the way.

The men just stopped in for lunch. This morning they caught one Mink and a beautiful Fisher worth about three hundred and fifty dollars. A worthwhile mornings catch. I hope they do as well this afternoon. There aren't many Fisher in this country but we've been lucky and have caught two so far.

I just went outside and knocked down some icicles so I can see out of the window. They were hanging from the roof right to the ground and although a pretty sight they did block the view.

It's a warm, sunny day today, almost perfect. Perfect for anything but trapping. It's plus thirty-eight degrees and there are even some mosquitoes out already. This is not what a person expects to find this far north this time of year. Yesterday while visiting the outhouse I saw a spider and some kind of moth.

No more weasel! We finally caught it in a trap. He kept trying to eat our dinner whenever I wasn't watching. At night he would jump out of a hole in the ceiling above my bed, land on my chest and run down my legs, then jump off the bunk and run across the floor to see what he could get into. We were scared that he would chew the furs that were drying around the cabin. All his goings on didn't disturb the men at all and they slept well while I kept watch as I couldn't come close to sleep knowing that as soon as everything was nice and quiet this thing was going to jump on me and run down my legs. I used to lie with a flashlight just waiting for him. It's not that he's not cute, but who wants a weasel for a sleeping partner!

We will be heading back to the small cabin soon to check on our traps there. I'll write more from there.

Feb. 1, 1984.
Hello again,
We're back at the small cabin again on route to Atlin. So far the trails have been drifted over in spots but otherwise pretty good. We're still doing a lot of snowshoeing. George does well what with having an artificial hip and all. I'm hard pressed to keep up with him for sure. You'd think I'd be nothing but skin and bone with all the exercise I've been getting but I guess that's just wishful thinking. We got one Mink and one Martin this morning and I hope we'll do as good this afternoon. We had just gotten the Mink when the funniest thing happened. We were crossing a stretch of lake where the overflow was usually bad so were crossing one by one. As Ted was breaking trail he went first and not having any trouble signaled for George to follow. As George pulled away and started crossing the lake I caught a movement out of the corner of my eye. Turning to look and see what it was, I was surprised to see a Mink running across the ice towards shore. Without thinking I dove off of my machine and grabbed the mink with my bare hands. When I realized that I had actually caught the thing I sure was surprised. Now all I had to do was figure out what to do with it before it decided to bite me. By this time both men were on the far side of the lake and signaling like mad trying to get me to follow them across. They were totally baffled by my strange actions as I decided that I would have to either kill this Mink or let it go before it hurt me. Holding on to its back end I decided to hit it's head hard against my snowmobile and proceeded to do so. The problem with this was I didn't want to hurt the animal and I guess my antics were quite hilarious as I battled with this Mink. Finally I proceeded across the lake to tell the men how good I was to have caught this wild Mink with my bare hands. It didn't take long for them to burst my bubble for when they looked inside the box where George had thrown the Mink we had gotten at the last trap it was empty. I guess it had been

unconscious and had come to and jumped out of the box just as George took off to cross the lake. They told me if it hadn't been drowsy I would have never been able to catch it. I told them they were just jealous as neither of them had ever caught a wild Mink with their bare hands.

Guess I'll say good bye and will mail this while I'm in town. I'll be glad to get a letter from your end too and always look forward to hearing the news from you.

Chapter 17

Strange Bedfellows

I was glad to get your letter while we were in town. We arrived back at Paddy Lake cabin two days ago and it's taken me two days to recuperate enough to write. The lakes were nothing but overflow and two feet of new snow lay on the trails. The men are out running the lines right now and should be back for lunch. The line they're running today is about four to five hours long barring any difficulties.

I had a nice break and stayed in town with Goldy for a week. The men went back to the line and as I didn't go Ted used my snowmobile instead of his own. Mine is smaller and easier on gas. Unfortunately, the bearing went in my machine while they were away and as usual we can't get a part for it in Atlin. So, I'm riding on the back of Ted's machine until the part for mine comes in. That made the trip back in here interesting to say the least, I thought we weren't going to make it for sure.

Ted's machine couldn't stay on top of the snow with two people on it plus the weight of the sled we were pulling, so we had to follow the old trails closely. As we've had lots of wind since the trails have last been used, it was hard to even find them never mind stay on them. We couldn't find a trace of them in the open spots. I tried riding on the sled instead of the back of Ted's machine but that was a total disaster as the sled kept tipping over and dumping me off and Ted would have to keep on going without me while I'd crawl on my hands and knees until we'd get to a stretch of old trail and the machine could hold both of us up again. Some of the lakes we were on were pretty long and it turned out that I did a lot of crawling. More than I've done since I learned how to walk. The crawling itself wasn't too bad but I had so many clothes on I could hardly walk never mind crawl. Finally we hit the end of Paddy Lake and sank out of sight in the over flow. It took us three hours to make a trail two hundred yards long so we could get the machines out of all the water. The entire three hours we were standing in water one and a half feet deep. As our boots are only one foot high, needless to say we were all soaking wet, cold, cranky and miserable. The temperature was just above zero. After all this, when we finally did get the machines to shore, Ted's machine wouldn't hold both of us up in the fresh snow again. The only solution was for Ted and George to go on to the cabin without me while I tried crawling again. This time I had a long ways to go. I tried lying down and rolling but found I couldn't make much headway this way so once again I started to crawl. Finally I hit a spot where the crust would hold me up and was able to walk for a ways and get the circulation going again in my wet feet. The men had left me with only one match and a hunk of fire starter for emergencies as one match was all that they could find. Everything else was on the sled still stuck in the overflow in the middle of the lake. I have never in my entire life felt as alone as I did then, literally standing in the middle of nowhere in zero degree weather, soaking wet and with only one match. I was cold, wet, and not in very good humor. I was sure glad to see Ted when he finally did return for me. When we finally reached the cabin George had gotten the fire going and it was starting to warm up our little home. Ted sat me down and pulled off my boots and socks and found that my insoles and socks were frozen to my feet, and my fingers and toes had a touch of frostbite. Other than that the three of us were all fine. When at long last we were all thawed out, Ted and George lay down and that left me to get supper. After we ate of course I was nominated to do the dishes, too.

The next morning bright and early the men went back for the sled and then ran the new line that we had snowshoed out. So far the line has been good to us and was a worthwhile endeavor. It's produced two Lynx, five Martin, and two Ermine. Lynx can bring as much as one thousand dollars each and are averaging around eight hundred right now. We shipped fifty-five Martin, two Fisher, four Coyote, eight Mink, eight Ermine, one Fox without a tail, and two Squirrel to the last sale in Vancouver. We hope they bring good prices, most northern furs usually do. We won't know how much each one brings until after the next fur sale.

On our last trip into Atlin, George had a hunk cut out of the top of his nose as he had a small spot of cancer there. Now he has a sore nose full of stitches to put up with on top of everything else.

It's windy and miserable out and is snowing like mad. We have about eight inches of new snow and it's hard to run the lines as the trails are all snowed under. We are doing a lot of reading and card playing lately.

Ted took George's stitches out this morning. His nose looks healthy and has healed well. As we didn't have any scissors, Ted had to saw the knots off with his pocket knife, then give the stitches a quick pull. George said the sawing hurt more than anything else. I can imagine as it hurt me just to watch the proceedings.

We had another pesky Weasel in the cabin again. Now we think we have a pack rat living under the floor. It's sure noisy in here when we're trying to sleep. All I can say is that I've had a lot of strange bedfellows this winter!

February 22, 1984

We still haven't been able to do much or to venture too far from the cabin because of the weather. We snow shoed up the mountain trail behind the cabin to check on some traps but didn't have any luck there. We've been doing lots of ice fishing and have been getting lots of lake trout all of them around four or five pounds. We're running out of books to read and will have to bring a new supply in on our next trip into town. We have played the same game of cards called *Nine-Five-Two* almost every night since we first arrived at the cabin, George hasn't won a game yet but is a good sport about it and keeps on trying.

The wind is still really strong. The other morning when we went out to the woodshed that's attached to the front of the cabin, we found a tiny owl sitting on a piece of firewood. He was only about six inches high and was all huddled over trying to keep warm. We figure that he was exhausted from trying to fight the wind and as the snows so deep and food so hard to come by, he was probably half starved too. We put some raw meat down for him but when we took a peek at him a few minutes later we found him lying on the floor dead. When Ted picked him up he said that he didn't weigh more than a few ounces he was so thin. We often see moose tracks in the snow now. They're sinking into the snow up to their chests. It's hard for them to find food as they have everything in reach eaten down already. It's even harder for them to keep away from the wolves when the snow is deep.

My thirty fourth birthdays only two days away, looks like no party this year.

We're going to head back to the other cabin and then into Atlin in the next day or so. As the weather has been so mild, the trapping hasn't been good lately. Hopefully we'll be able to make it to Whitehorse and pick up the parts for my machine while we're out. As soon as we get my machine fixed we're heading back in here to close everything up for this season. We're getting nervous that with the warm weather we've been having, the three big rivers between us and town will open up sooner than expected. If this happens we'll have to leave the machines here and snow shoe out. A distance of about sixty miles. I know the trip to the other cabin is going to be just awful tomorrow, especially since the two of us are riding double on Ted's machine. I'll probably end up on my hands and knees a lot again. Oh well, it keeps me humble anyway. I'll keep in touch and let you know how our trip goes.

    It's been a few days since my last letter and I wanted to let you know that we're back in town now. As things turned out, we managed to get everything closed up and arrived back in Atlin again with all of the usual problem and only one exception. There was a river about thirty feet wide that we had to cross between the small cabin and Atlin. This river is located at the bottom of a steep hill and directly on the other side of the river the ground rises sharply again. This particular spot usually doesn't cause too much of a problem when taken with enough speed, but this time the river was open. Although not deep, it slows the machines down quite a bit when you hit the open water and in order to make it up the far hill it was important to have lots of speed. After many futile attempts we decided that the only way we were going to make it was for me to stand on the far side of the river and as Ted flew past me, jump onto the back of his machine and hang off of the back end as far as I could to give him traction. This turned into an exciting ride for me and after about three or four tries we finally arrived at the top, amazingly enough all in one piece.
    Must say good-bye for now but will write more often now that we're at home again.

As the trapping season came to an end, we knew that we were going to miss the peace and tranquillity of the mountains and snow filled wilderness valleys in the winter season. We knew that we once again had been lucky enough to have experienced something that most people only dream of.

Out of our experiences grew a new respect for nature and for this winter wonderland, and the animals that dwell in it. The three of us had developed a special bond of friendship that comes from experiences, good and bad, that are shared together. We had fulfilled another of our life long dreams. We had faced another challenge of day to day survival and won.

Chapter 18

Spring Again

Spring found us once again in the mountains. We were miles from anywhere, with a pack string of horses, and, a new camp helper named Bob. Bob would help us cut trails, build camps, and later in the season, guide hunters.

Leaving Atlin with the pack string of horses, we rode as far as an old miner's cabin at Rose Creek the first night and set up camp. The horses behaved fairly well that day considering all they wanted to do was to turn around and head home again. We had had only one notable blow up when one of the horses disturbed a ground wasps' nest, then spooked the other horses, but for the most part, the ride through the long, buck brush covered valley was enjoyable.

As we rode along I studied the scarred landscape, a reminder of days when the price of gold was high and there were mines all through this area. Now, old mining cabins, settling ponds, rerouted streambeds, and broken down machinery were all that was left to tell the story.

Early the next morning, with the horses saddled and panniers redone, we set off, this time winding our way through miles of eskers, remnants of the glacier age. With blue skies above and the sunshine warming our bodies, the stress of everyday life slowly drained out of us. As the stillness of the wilderness overcame us we relaxed and knew this was where we belonged. We were at peace with ourselves and with everything around us. We know that we are of a privileged few that will ever experience this total feeling of peace and contentment.

As evening approached, we found ourselves at another tiny miner's cabin, this time at Bull Creek. Upon entering the cabin, we saw that the cabin's furnishings consisted of a set of rusty bed springs from a single size cot, its mattress long before destroyed by squirrels and mice. Beside the springs sat a wooden orange crate serving as a dresser. On top of the crate was a Cole oil lantern and a rusty tobacco tin full of wooden matches. Inside the orange crate was a supply of paperback books, their pages yellow with age. (Among them were those of Louis Lamour, which would be worth a fortune today.)

The cabin's one board that acted as a shelf boasted three more tobacco tins and upon further inspection I found one full of tea, the second half full of sugar cubes, and in the third a hand full of rice. A table made of faded boards sat in the middle of the room and a pop-up tin wood stove off to one side of the room complete the decor.

Neatly piled beside the stove was a pile of kindling and split firewood. In the morning we would replace whatever wood we used before we broke camp. The long ride in the fresh mountain air had tired us all out and it wasn't long until Bob rolled his sleeping bag out on the table. Ted and I had decided to share the cot springs and found out in a hurry that trying not to roll off onto the dirty floor was quite a feat. Once asleep we slept well and woke totally refreshed and ready to face another day's ride. Leaving the camp the way we found it, we set out early the next morning, headed towards Fox Creek. Fox Creek would be our last sign of civilization for quite a while. From this point on we would set up tent camps in the evenings or stay in the cabins at the hunting camps that we would be opening up for the season. Our only means of communication with the outside world would be by floatplane once in a while

At Fox Creek the country changed drastically into miles of bunch grass covered meadows, huge bottomless bogs, small lakes, treed valleys, and rugged mountain country.

The first bottomless bog that we crossed had me ready to turn tail and run for home. It's quite an experience tiptoeing from one clump of grass to the next leading a string of reluctant horses and at the same time keeping your fingers crossed that the grass will hold everything up. Once on the other side of the bog, the land changed again and we followed a twisted little creek through a grassy valley towards Line Lake. As it was only early June, parts of the creek were still frozen over and there were lots of snow drifts across parts of the trail. As we picked our way over ice bridges and through the drifts, we could see bright purple crocuses, the first wildflowers of the season, bursting forth in full bloom on all of the open grassy hillsides. In some spots the crocuses popped their heads up through the sparkling white snow and made quite the picture.

We had one more bog to cross and for this one we stayed on the horses' backs. The horses' lunged into the bog, and sank up to their chests in the mud and as they waded through, constantly tripped on submerged logs. I closed my eyes and hung on for dear life and was surely glad to reach solid ground again. Wet and cold, we were all more than happy when we crested the hill and in the distance saw Line Lake Camp. It didn't take us long to open one of the cabins, get a crackling fire going in the stove, and peel off all of our wet clothes.

The horses were glad to be in a corral once again as they were in need of a good rest. In this camp we would put bells on them and turn them loose to graze. This time of year when the horses are still fresh and there's lots of feed around for them they usually don't wander too far from camp. Later in the season, when they get tired and the grass has been all cropped close to the ground, sometimes finding them can be quite a chore. The more tired they get the smarter they get and sometimes Ted would find them hiding in the trees, standing with their chins tucked in tightly to immobilize their bells. Sometimes it took Ted a couple of hours to locate them and bring them back to camp in the mornings.

Chapter 19

Reflections

    Hello from Line Lake Camp, This morning as the men slept I wandered down the path to the dock. Sitting on a rock at the waters edge I sat quietly soaking up the beauty and peace of my surroundings. I found my mind wandering back through previous times spent in this camp.

    Looking ahead to the small bay across from where I sat I remembered the time when the hunters had been cleaning the day's catch of Greyling and one of the guides decided to take the gut pile over to the point on the far side of the bay and dispose of it there. We figured it would be far enough away not to attract any animals into the camp. It wasn't. No more than half an hour later when looking up from what we were doing we could see a big silver tipped grizzly bear feeding on the gut pile. The bear stayed until he finished the fish and then wandered off into the bush. What a rare sight to see! Opportunities like that don't come often.

    As I turned my head to study the lake's far shore my thoughts went back to the night we were all awakened by the sound of a pack of hunting wolves. We'd been keeping an eye on a cow moose and her twin calves for a couple of days so we had a pretty good idea what they were hunting. In the morning we set up the spotting scope at the edge of the lake and took a look around. On the far shore of the lake we could see the cow moose with only one calf left. The calf was totally exhausted and as the cow stood panting and trying to get her breath back, the calf lay down in the tall grass at her feet for a much-needed rest. As the cow stood guard and the calf rested, we could hear the wolves slowly working their way towards them. We kept an eye on them for a couple of hours and finally, as the wolves started to move in, the cow nudged her calf onto its feet and into the lake where both swam away to safety.

The willows to the left of me reminded me of the night as everyone slept peacefully in their tents, suddenly a racket brought me to a state of alertness. Amid the snores of hunters and guides, I could hear the grunting of a rutting bull moose outside of my tent. As he was fairly close to the tent we were sleeping in I woke up Ted up and told him to listen. Pulling on his longjohns he stumbled outside into the darkness to try and see what was going on. By this time the grunts were coming from near the edge of the lake so he decided to take a walk and try and get a look at the bull. Every once in a while Ted would grunt to get the bull's attention and the bull would grunt back. This way he would know where the moose was in the dark. Upon reaching the weedy area at the edge of the lake, Ted gave a grunt and much to his surprise, the bull grunted back from right beside him. Let me tell you there was a mad scramble as he hightailed it back to our tent. Much to our surprise none of the other guides or hunters heard a thing and snored peacefully on.

Looking back towards the cabin, where Ted was still sleeping, brought to mind the time when friends of ours were sleeping in the same cabin and were awakened by a lot of grunting and carrying on outside of it. Climbing up the wall to peek out the cabin's gable end that was covered in clear plastic, they could see a large sow grizzly and two cubs. They watched as the sow marched her two cubs down the trail to the dock and then proceeded to make them jump off the dock into the water and swim. If they didn't do what she wanted, she would give them a good swat with her paw and grunt quite loudly at them until they did. When the swimming lesson was over, all three marched back up the dock and followed the trail out of sight.

Even the dock brought back memories of the time when it had been really windy for a couple of days and as the lake was pretty stirred up, the fishing had been poor. Finally everything had calmed down and the hunters had decided to spend a peaceful afternoon fishing. Floating around a small bay about a quarter mile from camp, they were having pretty good luck and were catching some nice fish when, all of a sudden, one of them got a good strike and as he set the hook he knew he had a heavy fish on his line. Everyone waited with baited breath as he reeled his monster in and imagine their surprise when out of the water came a six pack of diet Coke. It had drifted away, from its hiding place, under the dock a quarter mile away in the previous storm. The chances of it ever being found must have been pretty slim.

In the background I was starting to hear the men moving around and knew it wouldn't be long before they would want their breakfast. It was time for me to leave the water's edge and get the fire going.

After spending a few days cleaning cabins and getting the season's firewood in, we once again saddled up the horses and set off down the trail. This time we were looking for a good spot to cut a trail through from Line Lake to Paddy Lake. We wandered around looking for a dry spot that we could put a trail through but realized that this particular bog ran right to the top of the mountain. In some spots the horses would refuse to cross it and in others they couldn't cross it. As we zigzagged our way through it, we eventually reached a drier area and came across part of an old blazed trail. We followed the blazes through the valley as it wound along a fast moving creek, swollen with run off water. In one shady spot where the trail crossed the creek we slid down the snow covered bank into the rapidly flowing water. Climbing back out on the other side up a boulder strewn bank was a really tricky feat. Soon the country changed and we found ourselves riding miles through a large, boggy, buckbrush covered valley that was covered in high willows. Setting up camp for the night in the high willows, we decided to return to Line Lake, then head back to Fox Creek and try to find a better spot to cut the trail through from that end.

After spending a few days at Line Lake and giving the horses a good rest, we set off back through the bogs and along the creek trail leading to Fox Creek. A couple of miles before we got there, we turned off the trail we were following and entered another small valley that would lead us towards Lost Lake, Mount McMaster, and eventually Langorse Lake. Setting up camp for the night, we all climbed thankfully into our sleeping bags as soon as we had eaten. As we lay listening to the silence around us, we could hear the horse bells ringing as they grazed peacefully close by and we drifted off to sleep.

The bells served many different purposes, not only did they tell us where the horses were, they warned other animals that the horses were around. If, while sleeping, one was awakened by all the horse bells ringing at the same time one would know that something had spooked them, probably a bear.

The next morning, with breakfast over, all the horses packed and lunches stowed safely in the saddlebags, we were on our way.

Bob had sold us one of the green horses in our pack string earlier this season. This particular horse turned out to be not only smart but pretty devious too. He had us worried for a while until we finally figured out what he was doing. We were riding along about mid-afternoon one day and had just finished crossing some rough country. The horses and riders were all pretty tired. As we crested a hill, in front of us we could see rolling green hillsides, tall shade trees, and a small lake. Upon approaching a wildflower covered meadow, suddenly there was a commotion and the pack horse that Bob sold us fell down and lay panting on the ground. Naturally we all jumped off of our horses and ran over to him to see what was wrong. Instantly, we stripped off his saddle and pack boxes, then inspected the horse closely. Not finding any outward sign of anything we decided he must be having a heart attack. Finally, we decided we didn't have much choice but to keep moving and leave the horse where he was. If he did survive his problem there was lots of fresh feed and water in this valley. As we rode away, I guess he figured out that he was getting left behind and jumping up, he ran up beside us and started grazing on the lush grass and prancing around, more than happy now that we had removed the heavy pack off of his back. We realized the horse had just outsmarted us. We decided he would pay for his deviousness the next day. We would put Bob on his back since it was his horse to start with. He would ride the horse and work it hard all day. About noon the next day, we came to a fairly narrow, long, deep bog hole that there was no way around and we had to cross. Ted's and my horses jumped with us on their backs and cleared the bog nicely but Bob's horse, being as lazy as he was, landed smack in the middle of the mud. We had a good laugh as horse and rider lunged their way through, both covered in wet, slimy mud. We told Bob it served him right for selling us a lazy horse in the first place, as late the night before he had finally confessed that he sold us the horse because it was lazy and he couldn't do anything with it.

 As we wandered through this mountain pass, the beauty of our surroundings held us all under its spell. Rolling grassy hillsides with a rapidly flowing, twisting stream wound its way through the valley. Farther along the trail we followed a spot where the stream was backed up by a big beaver dam, its banks overflowing onto the wildflower covered meadow. Fireweed, Monks Hood and Lupine grew in abundance everywhere we looked. In a distance we could see hillsides covered in tall timber and willows and the two or three different passes leading out of this valley. Now our problem was figuring out which pass to take.

 The first pass we chose looked like it might take us up into the high country and then over the top to Mount MCMaster. As luck would have it, we chose the wrong pass and finding ourselves back at the Beaver dam several hours later we decided to dismount and have lunch.

Our picnic in this peaceful spot gave us time to make new plans as to where we would head next. As we ate, we watched the Beaver as they busily went about their business as though we weren't even there.

Following a boulder strewn narrow pass between two high hills, we gradually climbed until we finally broke out into the lush, alpine meadow country. One lone Caribou rushed over to see what we were and, as if glad for the company, followed along behind the pack train for the rest of the day. When we made camp for the night, beside a glacial ice pack with a small run off stream flowing through flats covered in Arctic Cotton, our curious friend remained still close by, watching us.

The next morning, we set off again with our faithful follower still with us. It wasn't long before she was joined by two or three more caribou and shortly afterwards wandered away with them. As we approached a game trail leading down the Mountainside into Langorse Lake country, the view ahead of us was spectacular.

In the large valley ahead we could see two or three small lakes, including Paddy Lake off in the distance. This would be our destination. Beyond the valley lay range after range of snow-capped mountains, each with its own particular shape and shade of blue. As we slowly picked our way through the high willows that led down off of the mountainside, it wasn't long before we had to dismount and lead our horses through the tangled brush on foot. Walking was almost impossible in this thick brush and as we were all short tempered and extremely tired as the going was pretty tough. We were all glad when finally we found the trail leading to the tall timber country. As usual our sleeping bags looked pretty good to us by bedtime.

The next few days were spent trying to locate a stretch of old trail that wound its way through this enormous, bunch grass covered valley. We had to find the old trail as there was a wide stretch of deep bog running through the center of the valley and we needed to cross over to the other side of the valley. The problem we were having was that we kept loosing the trail in the same area no matter what angle from which we approached it. As soon as we came anywhere near the river that flowed through the middle of the meadow, the trail seemed to vanish. The area was full of deep bogs and upon reaching one big bog hole, we decided to stay on the horses' backs while they lunged their way through. I can remember trying to stay on my horse while she struggled across the bog hole with only her head showing. As this bog was the consistency of glue, It took all my strength and energy to keep from sliding off of her. As I was pulling the hesitant pack string along behind me with one hand, that left me only one hand to hang on with. I almost had heart failure when out of the corner of my eye I saw the panicking horse behind me jump into the bog hole, for as he jumped, both of his front hooves just missed my head by inches. Visions of the horse landing on top of me and drowning me in the mud flashed through my head. I don't know who was more nervous, the horse or me. In another bog Bob's horse sank almost out of sight with just her head sticking out. As this bog was a thicker consistency, we had to hook ropes on her and pull her out with our horses.

Later the same day, when both horses and riders were totally exhausted, the horse I was riding decided she wasn't going to listen to me anymore and that she was going to do exactly what she wanted. As some of the horses had spent the last twenty years in these mountains, Ted told me to let her go where she wanted and we'd watch her and see what happened. We all watched with our mouths open as she walked over to the river, stepped into the water, walked about five hundred yards upstream, and then, she, stepped out of the water and onto the old trail that we had spent all this time looking for, to continue her way without incident. I guess she finally just got tired of all our fooling around and decided enough was enough. It wasn't long until we had the rest of the horses across and were on our way, riding through the long, bunch grass covered meadow towards Bell Lake.

As evening approached we set up our camp on a hillside overlooking the lake. Sitting around the campfire, high on our hill overlooking Bell Lake, we watched a bull moose feeding on willows at the edge of the lake below us. As the tensions of the day slowly drained out of us, we became totally relaxed and at one with our environment and each other.

Early the next morning, as we drifted in and out of sleep, we could hear the Loons calling to each other on the lake below us. Once again it was time to climb out of our cozy bags. It didn't take long until we headed out, riding through miles of buck brush and boggy ground along the edge of Bell Lake towards Paddy Lake. This stretch of trail was hard going as both horses and riders were tired and cranky after being on the trail for so long. At one little creek, my horse decided she wasn't going to get her feet wet for anyone. I tried using the reins to make her move but she stood with her feet firmly planted on the dry ground. Neither standing in the creek, trying to pull her, or getting behind her and pushing her, moved her one inch. By this time, the men were tired and were getting pretty weary of all my fooling around so Ted got off his horse and walked back to where I was. Using his know how, it didn't take long to cross the creek and head down the trail.

The pouring rain didn't help anyone's disposition much either and by the time Paddy Lake cabin came into view we were all soaking wet, cranky, cold, hungry, and ready for bed.

Staying at the cabin for only one night, we left again early the next morning, this time headed for Rainbow Lake camp where we planned to spend some time resting the horses and opening up the camp for the season. Once there, we rested our weary bones. The fishing was good and we caught many small rainbow trout, and even caught some eastern brooks too. Great pan fish and good eating.

Chapter 20

Mountain Country

Once rested, we moved on down the trail leading to Dry Lake camp. As we followed bits and pieces of the Telegraph Trail, we came across many interesting remnants of times past. In one spot we followed a narrow stretch of corduroy road built many years ago. In another we rode past the remains of several falling down log cabins with their rotting log caches still balanced crookedly in the trees above them. Pieces of telegraph wire were scattered along the trail and we had to take special care that the horses didn't get any wrapped around their feet. The trail wound its way through the tall timber until breaking out into the open where we saw a steep bank directly in front of us and at the bottom of the bank, the dangerously swollen, fast moving, Nakina River. Wide and fast with its boulder strewn bottom it was a frightening sight. Knowing we were about to cross it on horseback, I was frozen with fear. As Ted led the way down the steep bank and coaxed his horse into the rushing water, horse and rider were caught in the current and swept downstream until the horse finally gained its footing and they slowly inched their way across to the other side. With my heart in my mouth and my eyes tightly shut I nudged my way forward down the steep bank and suddenly found myself in the cold water with my body submerged above my waist. I hung on for dear life as my horse righted itself and inched her way across, tripping and stumbling on the big boulders under the water. When we finally did reach the other side I was more than thankfull to be on dry land again.

Following another valley for the next fifteen miles, we entered a small grassy meadow and off in the distance could see our destination,

Dry Lake. We walked the horses to the meadow behind the camp, and staked them out to graze on the lush grass. After the horses were looked after, firewood was gathered and we soon had a crackling fire going. A quick meal of bannoch and beans was eaten. Then, setting up our camp for the night, we all climbed into our sleeping bags. It wasn't long before we drifted off to sleep listening to the horse bells tinkling in the distance.

Morning came early and we started opening up the camp for the season. When we tore the plywood covering off of the one storage tent the odor made us all sick. It looked like every porcupine in the area had wintered inside. What a mess! It took many pails of lake water and lots of bleach that was left over from the previous year to make it even bearable.

With the horses grazing contentedly on the first grass of the season, we took our time getting the camp prepared. To do this we had to set up the canvas wall tents. Each tent was set on its own individual log and board tent platform. The two foot high log walls were chinked with moss. Once the tents had been thoroughly cleaned inside and out, we cleaned and installed the tin, pop-up, wood heat stoves in the tents. The canvas cots had to be washed in the lake and set in the sunshine to dry before being put inside the tents. After that we installed a board table, two wooden benches and lots of shelves inside the kitchen tent. The outhouse was the next project and usually had to be repaired and often a new hole scratched out of the rocky ground. After the camp was ready, we had another big job ahead of us. We had to cut and split enough firewood for the season, then, haul it back to camp in pack saddles on the horses backs. This particular camp sat right at tree line and any fire wood that was needed had to be hauled from a half mile away. Not only had the horses earned a well deserved rest but so had we.

After a day of relaxing we saddled up the horses and headed out to cut some new trails and check on some older ones. Following an old game trail from camp through the valley where the horses had been staked out, we came to a small crystal clear pond. Here, we turned into another valley and followed it towards distant Nakina Lake. A couple of miles later we crossed to the far side of the vivid green valley and started to climb. As we rode peacefully along we passed through miles of monks hood, lupin and wild columbine. The air was heavy with the scent of wildflowers. We followed glacier run off streams with their edges covered in Arctic cotton, and picked our way through debris left over from long ago slides that left huge bald scars on the mountain sides. Leaving this valley we found ourselves climbing steeply, the trail passing through thick bushy spruce trees and crisscrossing a swollen fast moving creek.

It wasn't long until we came to a rickety old foot bridge that consisted of a couple of boards that someone in the distant past had placed across a deep ravine. The creek rushed by far below. Crossing the bridge was nerve racking for the horses as well as for the riders and we were all glad to get to the other side. Once across, it was only a few miles farther until the trail broke out into the high Alpine country and following a game trail to a secluded little cirque, an isolated little valley high in the mountains, we set up camp.

The cirque was the perfect camping spot consisting of a small stream that would supply our water, a ring of trees that would supply our firewood and protection from the elements and tall lush grass along the streams edges for the horses grazing. Early the next morning we staked out the pack string so they wouldn't follow us and left to investigate the area above our cirque.

Following a well used game trail, we headed along the edge of the cirque, climbing rapidly then reaching a plateau from where miles of high Alpine country was visible to us. Covered in caribou moss and six-inch high buck brush with a picturesque mountain lake off in the distance, the country ahead of us had a special kind of beauty. Usually there are sheep grazing on the rolling hillsides around where we stood, but this particular day we didn't see any and decided to go for a ride to investigate the area above our cirque. Returning to camp we saddled up our horses and rode to another hidden cirque where we dismounted, staked out the horses and quietly approached it. Among the boulders on the cirque's grassy edges were some of the largest goats any of us had ever seen. All, except the youngest one, looked like they would set new Boone and Crocket records. They were so big when they walked they swayed like a big old grizzly bear. Later in the season we brought a bow hunter here. He shot the smallest of the goats and set a Pope and Young record with it. That shows just how big the others must have been.

After a couple of days rest we saddled up the horses and left to investigate the mountain to the right of camp. We planned to wander through the high country and eventually end up in sheep camp. One evening we came across a fairly deep valley and looking down we could see the perfect camping spot for the night, located beside a pretty little stream that meandered through the valley and was set amid gnarled, twisted, stunted trees. The slopes leading into the valley were so steep we knew it would be tricky getting the horses down into it. Dismounting we decided to lead them over the edge and down. The only problem with this idea turned out to be that in order to lead them we had to be in front and below them and constantly had to dodge boulders and dirt that they were knocking down on top of us.

Once at the bottom it didn't take us long until we had all the tents set up and supper cooking over a crackling campfire. As we all relaxed we enjoyed watching the horses graze contentedly on the tall grass that grew in abundance along the creeks edge. In the morning as we packed up the camp and prepared to leave, I was sorry to go and wished all of our camping spots were as perfect as this one.

Descending into the valley had been hard, but as we left we had to lead the horses up the steep hills surrounding the valley. About half way up I tired and couldn't move another step. Ted noticed my predicament and hollared back to me to get into the middle of the pack string and hang on to the tail of the horse in front of me while pulling the rest of the horses along behind me. This worked perfectly as the horses were used to pulling each other when times got tough. When we arrived at the top I wasn't even puffing and being pulled along with the pack string was a whole lot easier than trying to go the rest of the way on my own.

As we wandered through this beautiful country we saw many snowy white mountain goats and elusive sheep. I took lots of good pictures of all of the animals. We enjoyed this time together, for we knew that soon there would be lots of hunters around and another guiding season would be in full swing,

Chapter 21

Goat Hunting

August 18, 1984.
Dear Mom Dad,
    Here we are in Rainbow Lake hunting camp. The first two days our hunters were here, it poured rain and we couldn't leave the camp. On the third day, it cleared up and looked like it was going to be a nice day so we headed up the mountain. Of course all the rain had left the steep trail we were following nice and slippery and we had quite a time.
    Once on top, the country we were in was covered in goats. We saw a total of over sixty goats on this hunt and got up to within thirty feet of one while it fed We were able to study it for quite a while. As it wasn't big enough to shoot, we had fun just watching it. This was a once in a life time experience as goats are very illusive creatures and are found in the most difficult of terrains.
    The four of us had just crested a small hill when suddenly Ted signaled for us to keep still and be quiet. From the position Ted was in he could see a goat headed towards us just over the rise. We all froze and an unbelievably magical thing happened.

With the wind blowing towards us, the goat had no idea we were there and walked up to within thirty feet of us and stood looking around. What a sight this majestic animal was as it stood alone, in perfect sight of us, grazing on the thick green grass while we sat and watched. We were all dying to take pictures but knew that with the slightest movement the goat would be gone. Suddenly, something must have made it suspicious and the goat did the funniest thing. Turning its back to us it started to graze on the carpet of luscious grass at it's feet. Every once in a while it would lift it's back foot and scratch behind it's ear, all the while watching us slyly as if trying to catch us moving. Eventually, convinced that all was well, the goat slowly wandered off over the hill grazing as it went. As we moved forward so we could peer over the hill, we were able to see the herd directly below us, and our female hunter was able to get a good shot off and was lucky enough to get a nice goat. After three more days of pretending that we were goats as we climbed around the mountains, we arrived, back at Rainbow Lake camp with two trophy goats and four tired people.

Today we are resting but tomorrow we will venture back up Granite Mountain again, this time after sheep.

When we headed back down the mountain to camp, we decided to leave some of our gear on top so that we didn't have to turn around and pack it all the way back up again in a few days. We left two tents standing and in the one tent the hunter left his custom made rifle and expensive camera. We stored all the extra gear in ours. This made our descent much easier. A few days later upon our arrival back on top, we found that a wind had come up and had blown the hunter's tent and its contents away. Finally, locating the tent over the side of the mountain, we investigated and discovered that its contents were all okay. We rebuilt the camp and all fell thankfully into our sleeping bags.

Early the next morning when we crawled out of

our tents, we found that clouds had rolled in during the night making it impossible to see more than three feet in any direction. As we were on the very tops of the mountains, the clouds were often lower than we were. The clouds stayed with us for two or three days causing everyone to be restless, cranky and itching to get out hunting.

On the second day we took a vote and decided that it looked like the clouds were going to lift and that we would hike back into the area where we planned to hunt for sheep. That way we would have a head start when the clouds finally did lift. The four of us set out in single file but before long we found that the clouds were getting thicker again and we couldn't see a thing. Leaving a trail of small cairns made of piles of stones, we headed in what we thought was the right direction and found ourselves going around in circles. As we knew this area of the mountains well, we never carried a compass with us. This was one time we could have used one. After many hours of this we finally ended up back at our tents thanks to Ted's good sense of direction. The next morning we headed down the mountain empty handed but thankful that we were all okay.

We are back in camp with the last hunt over and the camp empty of hunters for a few days. Ted and I are taking advantage of the peace and quiet and are having a good rest We've seen two or three moose on the lake almost every day but don't have time to take care of the meat properly if we shoot one for ourselves, as we are expecting more hunters any time now.

The porcupines are keeping us awake at night as they are trying to eat the plywood floors in the cabin. If one lies quietly in bed at night and listens to the porkies, one will hear first one animal start to gnaw on the wood. A few moments later the single porkie will bark and call in the other porkies to help him eat everything in sight that has salt in it.

The moose are on the move, and yesterday I saw

six different ones from the cook tent. They are always fun to see and to take pictures of.

    A year or so later Ted and I on another hunt on Granite Mountain, came across the rock cairns we had left on the mountain during our trip in the clouds. We decided to follow them to see where we had been and discovered that in one spot we had come within just a few feet of a sheer rock drop off on the edge of the mountain. In another spot we had wandered out on a grassy point that was surrounded by sheer rock cliffs then had turned and headed back off the point into a meadow. After seeing where we had been that day, if it looks like the clouds are going to descend on us, we stay in camp. We were lucky to have escaped without anyone falling off of the mountain. I think our Guardian angels were working overtime that day.

Chapter 22

Backpacking

It's July and we are in Rainbow Lake camp, time sure flies. Rainbow Lake is a pretty little lake with a new camp on it that consists of a board cabin with a kitchen, sitting room area and a bedroom at one end for the guide and cook. There are two new wall tents with plywood walls and floors that serve as sleeping quarters for the hunters. The plywood was flown in on the floats of the Beaver float plane.

This camp sits on the edge of Rainbow Lake and is surrounded by rugged mountains where we'll be hunting for goats and sheep. We are at about thirty-five hundred feet here. The out house in this camp is always a popular spot as while one sits and contemplates life, the view of the lake and mountains is amazing. We always look forward to an early morning trip. Many times in the early mist I have heard moose grunting or have watched them playing and feeding on weeds at the lake's edge. We've had a cow and calf moose on the lake early each morning for the last week.

On this particular trip we stayed in Rainbow Lake for over a week. We spent many hours relaxing and fishing and caught lots of Eastern Brooks Trout and small Rainbows.

```
We backpacked the camp supplies to the top of
Granite Mountain so that when our hunters arrive
everything will be ready for them. We won't be
using horses on this hunt as one of the hunters is
allergic to them. Packing the supplies to the moun-
tain top turned into quite a chore. The narrow,
winding, overgrown trail that heads up Granite
Mountain starts off as a nice easy hike but before
long we found ourselves in bogs and willows. At one
time the trail had been a small creek but in years
past the stream had gone underground leaving this
trail of boggy ground to follow. Farther along,
the trail climbs almost straight up and is a real
workout especially with heavy packs on our backs.
I know if the mountains were even ten feet higher
I wouldn't have made it to the top. Ted had to
ferry the gear up and down the last twenty feet as
it was, I just couldn't move another step without
a rest. This body will only do so much, then it
quits. Having the will to do more doesn't always
help. I still haven't figured out if I'm having fun
yet or not.
```

I found out later, that as we followed the last half mile or so of trail to the mountain top, we had also been following fresh grizzly bear tracks that had been made by a large bear. Each time Ted saw a track he would step on it so that I wouldn't know that it was there. We were glad that we never did stumble onto the bear.

Upon reaching the top of Granite Mountain the breathtaking scenery surrounding us made the hard climb more than worthwhile. Range after range of majestic snow capped mountains, each one a different shade of blue. Sparkling white glacier ice packs with their milky blue run off ponds each nestled in vivid green Alpine valleys were visible as far as the eye could see. Wild Columbine nodded their heads in the breeze, their scent heavy in the air. Mountains in Alaska, the Yukon and British Columbia, could be seen from this one vantage point.

Behind me lay Rainbow Lake and the camp we had left early this same morning. Off in the distance a corner of Paddy Lake where we had spent the winter on the trap line was visible through the mountain valleys. To my right in the distant haze I could see the scar of the old Sloko burn, and over my shoulder the southern tip of Atlin Lake. To my left lay the rugged, remote, Nakina Lake area and Dry Lake hunting camp. Ahead of me lay the coastal mountains, the Taku drainage, and far off Alaska. The extraordinary beauty of this spot never fails to fill me with a sense of wonder, awe and thankfulness at having had the opportunity to experience its spell.

As we approached the mountain's edge, a shallow valley leading to another peak became visible. Lying on the ground side by side, together we lazily watched a herd of mountain goats grazing in the Alpine valley in front of us. This herd consisted mainly of nanny's, kids and some young Billy's. To be within two-hundred yards of a herd of wild mountain goats is an unforgettable, exciting experience. Naturally our cameras were put to good use capturing on film the frolicking young kids and watchful Nannys.

One big dry Nanny seemed to be totally in charge with groups of youngsters being tended by a few older helpers much like a nursery school. Later in the day, once our camp had been set up and we were ready for the night, we set up our spotting scope and watched the goats on another hillside for a while longer.

In the morning before heading back down the mountain to Rainbow Lake, we secured the camp. Perishables were hung in trees from a rope to keep them out of the reach of any animals. We wrapped everything that would fit in a waterproof tarp and raised it high in the trees branches. It was time now for us to say good-bye to this special place and head back down the mountain.

Upon our return to camp we found out by the radio that our backpack hunters had been delayed for a couple of weeks. We decided that instead of climbing all the way back up the mountain and packing the camp back down that we would leave everything where it was and keep our fingers crossed that the animals wouldn't destroy anything until our return.

The next day the drone of the float plane could be heard long before it became visible and dropped down to land on our little lake. Ted and I climbed on board and our next stop was remote Nakina Lake. There we met two hunters, fed them lunch, and got them on their way to Dry Lake camp with a guide and a pack string of horses.

Ted and I spent the night in a small two man nylon tent on the edge of Nakina Lake last night while we waited for the Super Cub float plane to arrive and drop off Sherman, the photographer, who going to spend some time in camp with us taking pictures for a book that he was making about this area.

At one time in the distant past, Nakina Lake was an Indian camping ground and the area has seen few humans except the local natives, odd trapper or local hunter. The previous year the Dry Lake area was opened up for hunting by the outfitter. The entire area was crawling with grizzly bears. Everywhere we looked we could see the tracks of various size bears

Early this morning we watched a fair sized bull moose feeding and playing in the water at the edge of the lake. We were totally mesmerized by his performance as he would submerge his head and when he lifted it again the sun would turn all the cascading water droplets into tiny rainbows of color. He was a magnificent creature and put on quite a performance for us.

Shortly after Sherman's arrival the three of us set off down the trail with our pack string of horses that the guide from Dry Lake camp had left us the previous day. Our eight hour ride along the Telegraph Trail ended when we finally arrived in Dry Lake camp. What a ride we had! Believe me when I say that pack trains and long trips sound like far more fun then they are in reality. On this trip we ended up with a bunch of green horses that kept bucking the packs off, breaking the pack saddles and then stampeding through the bushes. Of course every time this happened all of the horses had to be rounded up and then repacked. During one of these blow ups, we had to cut a green horse loose from the rest of the string. This horse was never seen again. One of the younger horses kept spooking at everything and would try and hide behind Ted for protection. The country we were riding through was pretty rugged, sometimes, the horses sunk up to their stomachs in bog holes or they would slip and fall crushing our legs against the trees. Some parts of the trail were straight up and down and were so steep it was hard to stay on the horses' backs. In some places I was so scared I closed my eyes, hung on tightly and prayed. The trail we were following zigzagged back and forth across a small river the whole way following ravines and cliffs. After a long hard days' ride we were all more than glad to see camp.

Upon our arrival in camp we discovered our friend Jan and her two young boys of about five and eight. Her husband Ed was one of the Dry Lake camp guides and she was the camp cook. It was always nice to see another female.

Ted another guide and two hunters left to go sheep hunting. They will stay at sheep camp in the high country for three or four days. To get to the camp, one rides through miles of lush rolling Alpine meadows that are covered in many species of wildflowers. The camp itself is set in a small cirque that contains a few gnarled trees and a small pool of glacier runoff water. Across from the camp, about one-hundred yards away, are rock cliffs with three or four small caves high in their sides. We've found that in really hot weather the sheep tend to stay in these caves to take advantage of the coolness they offer.

We knew that Sherman would get many beautiful pictures on this trip. Hopefully, the hunters would be able to get a trophy sheep too. With the men out of camp for a few days, that left Jan, her two children and myself.

Last night Jan and I were running around outside in the dark shooting porcupines four different times. One person would hold the disposable flashlight while the other shot the porkie. I'm sure we must have looked pretty silly as here we were, two woman alone in the middle of the mountains, dressed in men's long johns, running around in the dark with a disposable flashlight shooting porcupines. There have been over forty shot in this camp alone so far this season. They have to be destroyed as they can eat a leather saddle in a matter of minutes. In this camp they have eaten just about all of the top half of the out house. They love anything with salt in it. They are so destructive that as soon as we hear them, we grab a flashlight and start looking for them. It's bad enough being way out here with no men around, never mind wandering around in the dark shooting porcupines with a little .22 rifle.

The last time we were in this camp the guys saw a total of twenty-two different grizzlies. So far we haven't seen any but I've been sleeping with one eye open and a loaded gun by my side.

Our weather has been exceptionally warm and we've dammed up the glacial creek that runs through camp and made a swimming hole for the kids. Normally the creek is about twenty feet wide and one foot deep. Now that it's dammed up, some spots are about three feet deep. You know it's hot when glacier water feels good. There are many, many black flies and mosquitoes around. There's also lots of horseflies and they are ferocious biters.

I'll be glad when the men return as it's lonesome without them. Hopefully they'll get a nice sheep. The sheep and goats will be hard to hunt in this heat as they have moved lower and are hiding in the timber where it's cooler. There are lots of caribou around but the season isn't open for them.

We've just finished eating and putting the kids to bed. It's still beautifully sunny and there's a warm breeze. There are no clouds in sight and it looks like another beautiful day tomorrow. Having weather like this, this high up is rare as it's usually rather cold by now.

I did the laundry in the creek yesterday and no matter how warm the air was the water was still freezing cold on the hands. There are dozens of Arctic ground squirrels around this year and they aren't scared of anything. They come right into the cook tent looking for hand-outs. The kids are leading them around on strings. They have gotten so tame, the kids have named them after all the different hunting camps. They catch them by setting a snare made out of string over their burrow holes and when they pop their heads up the kids

```
pull the noose light and snare them.
    Time for bed now but I'll continue this letter
the first chance I get.
```

    The next morning as we were getting out of our cozy sleeping bags, I had a run in with a Grizzly bear as told in the August twenty-eighth letter I wrote to my Mom and Dad. I did not tell my parents at the time that it happened as I didn't want to worry them. I was waiting to find out the total amount of damage that I had done to my face with the rifle I had used.

Chapter 23

Grizzly

August 28, 1984
Dear mom and dad,
　　Thought I'd bring you up to date on the news. Guess it's about time that I tell you of my terrifying experience with a Grizzly bear. It happened while the men were in sheep camp and Jan and I were running around in the dark shooting porcupines. One night about midnight, a porkie decided to crawl under my tent frame and eat the plywood floor. Once we shot the porkie he got wedged between the ground and the plywood floor. As it was dark we decided to wait until daylight to try and get him out. Once back in bed the strong musky odor of the porcupine made it impossible to sleep, so, I decided to share the tent with Jan and the kids on the other side of the creek. Grabbing my sleeping bag, I hurried across the board walkway that spanned the creek and climbed into the tent where Jan and the kids were sleeping. It wasn't long until we were all sound asleep. During the night we were disturbed several more times by the gnawing noises made by the porkies as they tried to eat our surroundings and as usual we jumped out of bed and took care of the problem. At daylight when we felt something bump into our tent we took for granted it was just

another porkie and rolling over went back to sleep. Not long after that Jan got up went outside and started chopping firewood to get the fire in the cook tent going. Thomas, Jan's oldest son, went outside to go to the washroom and to give me some privacy to get out of my sleeping bag. As I was crawling out of the sleeping bag I heard this little voice outside of the tent saying mom, mom, quick, there's a grizzly out here. As I ran for the tents' exit I grabbed the closest rifle to me. Unfortunately for me it turned out to be a 7 mm magnum. By this time the bear was about fifty feet away from us and was getting pretty excited. He was scooping up dirt with his powerful front feet and popping his jaw as he charged towards us. Not too sure what we should be doing about our circumstances we talked it over quickly and decided to let the grizzly wander around camp and feed on dead porkies in the hopes that he would wander off on his own. It didn't take long for us to figure out that he wasn't going to leave on his own and that he was getting more and more agitated as time went by so, we decided we didn't have much choice, we had to do something about him. As Jan grabbed my rifle and took a shot at the bear he stood up on his hind legs and roared. Thinking that Jan had wounded him I fired the 7 mm magnum. Being above tree line and not having any kind of a rest for the gun, I didn't realize how much kick the rifle would have when I fired it and the recoil sent the rifle and scope back into my face and eye. It did a lot of damage. When it hit my face a flap of skin fell down over my right eye and I couldn't see the bear for skin and blood. Both of us thought my eye had fallen right out of the socket. The kids were more upset over the blood than the bear and one of them ran into the cook tent, climbed up on the stove and grabbed a tea towel for me to hold over my face. Meanwhile, during all the confusion the bear ran merrily over the mountain. That left me, miles from anywhere, eight hours by horseback to the closest lake that a float plane could land on, with my head bleeding, swelling and totally numb. My eye was swollen shut and there were two big sacks of blood hanging on my cheeks. We lifted up the flap of skin to make sure my eye was still there and not being too sure of the extent of the damage, we decided to tape butterfly bandages over the cut to hold it together. Then we protected the damaged eye by covering it with a cloth. Both of us then sat on guard watching for the wounded grizzly bear to return. We thought he would probably circle around and come back on us after dark, if not before. At this point we were pretty worried about spending another night in a tent with two children and a wounded grizzly running around, so we both sat down and started to pray. It wasn't long after that Ted and his hunters rode into camp a few days early with our only radiophone.

Ted right away radioed into the Red Cross station in Atlin and talked to the nurse. She phoned into Whitehorse and talked to a doctor and was told that I needed to get into Whitehorse Hospital right away for tests as there was no feeling at all left in my head and all I could hear was a loud ringing in my right ear. This was much easier said than done. Luckily, a helicopter pilot that was hauling fire fighters back and forth to a fire in the mountains picked up Ted's conversation with the nurse on the radio and said if we could guide him to where we were he would pick me up and take me into Atlin. We were all glad to hear this, especially me as my head certainly hurt. Just to add to the confusion, the lake we were camped on wasn't marked on any map so Ted had to give him the best directions he could. When the helicopter got close enough for us to hear it, Ted talked the pilot into our little valley and the rest of the way into camp. The worst part of all this was that the weather was extremely bad as usual and the ceiling was only about 500 feet. What a ride out through the mountains we had.

Once in Atlin I had to arrange for a friend to drive me into Whitehorse Hospital and I didn't arrive there until about three-thirty the next morning.

  Here's a list of the damages done but don't start worrying as I really am okay. I broke my nose and cracked open both of my sinuses, breaking the bone beside the right one. When the sinuses closed again, they closed on the nerve from my eye. I cracked my jaw and severed two other nerves in my face. I also have a cut two inches long and to the bone in my eyebrow, a perfect match for the round eye piece of the scope I was looking through. Needless to say that ended my porcupine shooting career to say nothing of grizzlies. I figure now that I've made it this long I'm sure to survive so, like I said, don't start worrying needlessly. Ted took a picture of my face before I left camp in the chopper so I'll send you one as soon as it's developed. Now, Ted has the baby face in our family and I look like I belong in the bush. The doctor said it will be six or eight months before he'll be able to tell the full extent of the damage. Besides having a bad headache and an aching jaw, I still have two black eyes and a lot of bandages. Our hunters are almost scared to fire their big rifles since they've seen me. Oh well, it gives everyone something to talk about. Now don't start worrying as I'm just fine. I have already backpacked all over Granite Mountain with our sheep and goat hunters a week after happened so I figured it was about time to tell you.

  Must close and will send this letter out with the next plane. Hope everyone at that end is okay. I'll try a get a picture of my face off to you so you can see for yourselves that I really am fine.

Chapter 24

Fire Mountain

Hi, As you can see we're in a different camp since I last wrote to you. We flew into Line Lake camp for a few days, then left there with two new hunters and headed for the high country.

Our hunters are a husband and wife team, about the same age as we are. We've been enjoying their company. Jim is after a caribou and his wife Deborah isn't hunting and just came for the holiday. Dick and Holly are guiding Deborah's parents who just returned from hunting in Africa.

The horseback ride to Fire Mountain usually takes about eight hours assuming that all the pack horses behave and we don't have any major blow ups. Leaving Line Lake, we followed a valley trail that winds its way along a small river and then crosses the river on top of a beaver dam. We followed the trail along the far side of the river for another hour until we came to the Rapid Roy River and crossed it. An interesting thing happened just before we got to the second crossing. We were riding along the trail in single file relaxing and enjoying the scenery when Ted looked up and saw a Wolverine coming down the trail heading straight for us. He was moving fast and with his head down and the direction that the wind was blowing he had no idea at all that the trail ahead of him was occupied by us. Ted let out a loud shout to warn him of our presence and stopping short he raised his head to see what was going on and took off with out farther ado into the bushes just in time to avoid a confrontation with the horses. Wolverines pound for pound are one of the most fierce animals anywhere.

After the river crossing, we came to a large, open natural meadow with a couple of weathered board sheds and a falling down log outhouse sitting off to one side. The remains of an old gold mining camp from the Klondike gold rush. Over the years anyone that took a notion to mine in the river close by, used this area as a base camp.

We left the valley and started to climb up towards the high country. Looking back over my right shoulder I could see an old wooden ore cart sitting on a stretch of rusty track far below in the rocky ravine. Imagine how much work it must have been to get these items into this isolated area where now-a-days the closest road is still forty miles away. Back in the days of the Klondike Gold rush there were no roads and these items would have been brought in by dog sled. What a job! The particular stretch of trail that we were following has some tight corners and some sections that are extremely steep. When wet the ground is slippery and quite treacherous. We were always glad when we reached higher ground and the trail broke out into the open. It was then a beautiful ride through a small valley with its buck brush and willow covered sides. Once while riding through this same valley during the rutt, we watched a bull moose with his herd of cows but on this trip all was quiet around us.

A few miles farther and we were in the high country where herds of caribou abound. About this time the weather turned miserable and the remaining five or six hours of riding was done in the pouring rain, strong winds, hail, and even some snow. Camp was a most welcome sight when it finally came into view.

Fire Mountain camp reminds me of Dog Patch from the comic books. It sits at forty-seven hundred feet and is the highest altitude of any of our base camps. It has always been my favorite camp as it's so unique. Originally built as a mining exploration camp, in years past it was used by geologists that were testing for iron in this area. The camp consists of two wooden shacks joined together in the center by a board walkway. One side of the shack has two board bunks attached to a wall and the other side is a makeshift kitchen that consists of a rickety wooden table, a couple of backless stools made out of weathered boards, a rusted pop-up stove for heat and a small board cupboard. At some time in the past a grizzly bear had entered the cabin through its one and only window so it was boarded up to keep out the elements.

When this camp was built, all the building supplies were flown in by helicopter. As we are a long way above tree line here, there is no firewood, so we burn the 2x4s remaining of the original camp buildings. The rest of the lumber has been put to good use over the years as well. The horse corrals, made entirely out of different colored doors, is quite a sight.

The outhouse here is a real experience to use. It's built out of two old pieces of plywood propped together in an A-frame style. A steel cable runs across the top of both anchoring the whole thing to the ground so it doesn't blow away in the strong winds that are so frequent up here. To use the outhouse you have to lower your clothing outside and then back into it already in a sitting position, for once inside there's no room left to move at all.

There are lots of caribou in this area, in fact one night while sitting at the table playing cards, one more curious than the others, stuck its head in the door to see what we were doing. One time when Ted staked out the horses for the night, there were both sheep and caribou on the same hillside where he put the horses. They were still there grazing contentedly in the morning when he returned to get the horses. The animals aren't used to seeing humans and are curious.

As every saddle was equipped with saddle bags where the lunches were carried, everyone could eat whenever he got hungry during the day. Even the horses got to know where the food was carried and if we weren't careful they would steal our lunches out of the saddle bags as we rode along. Some of the horses loved moose meat sandwiches and chocolate bars.

Finally with everything ready for the day we headed away from camp through a valley surrounded by rolling hillsides and covered in low lying buck brush and caribou moss. Every once in a while we could see caribou skylined on the distant horizon. Once we came across a fair sized bull caribou and Jim decided that he wanted to shoot it in case he didn't see another one. Ted didn't think it was large enough to shoot as it was still early in the hunt and chances were that we would see a bigger one if we waited. With great difficulty we talked Jim into waiting for a larger animal. Jim still wasn't too sure he should wait and as the day wore on with no more caribou in sight, he was getting more and more upset with Ted until things got to the point where he wasn't talking at all. On any other day by this time we would have seen lots of caribou, but this day we had no luck at all. As Deborah and I rode along behind the men teasing Jim for pouting laughing and having a good chat, Ted suddenly signaled Jim to keep us quiet. We were approaching a small valley and as we crested the hill, in front of us lay a herd of about fifty caribou. Jumping off of their horses the men lay flat on the ground deciding which animal they were going to shoot. Finally, deciding on the big light colored herd bull, Jim shot and the rest of the herd ran off only to return a short time later looking for their leader. It wouldn't be long though before they would regroup and choose a new one.

```
Our hunter got a nice caribou on his hunt. While
the men worked on the animal getting it ready for
transport, the entire herd stood around watching
from just a short distance away. One young bull
caribou with a broken off horn spotted me and
walked over to investigate. I had a great time
playing hide and seek around a big rock with him
for a good hour. He was only about ten feet away
from me as we played. I have some great pictures of
all these goings on that I'll send you.
```

Jim was no longer pouting and was once again talking to everyone. He was more than happy now that Ted had told him to wait for a larger animal. The caribou that Jim shot made the Boone and Crocket record book. I would have hated to see what would have happened had we not seen another caribou that day.

Bonnie Traplin

Chapter 25

Desolation Lake

Hello,
Hope by now you've received my last couple of letters. This will probably be the last one I'll be writing to you until we get back into town. It won't be long until hunting season is over again for this year.
We are in a different camp again and are roughly four hours by horseback from Fire Mountain camp. We left Fire Mountain early one morning and headed down a peaceful little valley towards Desolation Lake. As we rode through the valley we enjoyed the spectacular scenery surrounding us. On our left were green Alpine meadows and miles of gently rolling hills covered in caribou moss and two foot high florescent red buck brush. On our right the country was quite rugged with a small glacier blue mountain lake ringed with snow capped mountains off in the distance. It wasn't long though before the trail ended suddenly and as we exited the narrow rocky pass we were going through we suddenly we found ourselves walking across a small glacier. As we crossed the glacier we followed the tracks made by a small herd of caribou, I hung on to the saddle horn, held my breath closed my eyes

and prayed that I didn't sink out of sight in the
snow. Once across we descended into another valley
and rode peacefully along spotting small groups of
caribou and putting our cameras to good use. From
the time we left Line Lake until we reached Desolation Lake we saw well over one hundred caribou.
They are curious creatures. We had some run right
up to our pack string of horses as if trying to
figure out what the strange caravan was that was
passing through this isolated area.

    One time, in the excitement of seeing the horses and riders, a herd bull and his harem of cows became separated from each other, some of them running to our right and the rest to our left. It was interesting to see the way the bull took part of the herd to a safe spot and returned for the rest of his herd.

We are lucky to be able to see things that most
people will never get to see and to be able to
study all the different wildlife that live in this
remote area in their natural habitat. The scenery
has been an added bonus. With the buck brush in
fall colors its been an exceptionally beautiful
trip.

    A little farther along the trail we left the caribou behind us and let the horses pick their way through rugged rocky mountainsides, huge jagged boulders, bottomless bogs and twisted gnarled stunted trees. This stretch of trail was always hard on both horses and riders and we were glad when the trail once again broke out into rolling hills and meadows and we once again found ourselves in caribou country.
    Desolation Lake camp is built on a small lake set high on the mountain at tree line. The lake itself is a small treacherous lake to land or take off of in any plane larger than a Super Cub. In order to take off one has to head into the prevailing wind that comes out of the mountain valley. After lift off you must gain enough altitude to clear a ridge while turning away from the mountain, all the time holding your breath that you don't hit a down draft that could result in a dangerous loss of altitude at

a critical moment. This happened to the **B**eaver on if s first trip out with passengers and made for a very exciting flight.

The trees here are gnarled and stunted and are hundreds of years old. The camp is new this year and consists of a nice cabin that has two bedrooms, with a kitchen in the middle. There are two new tent frames and of course an outhouse again with a perfect view of the lake and the valley where the horses graze, when they are not in use. In this camp we will hobble the horses at night and let them loose to graze in the day time.

Once, one of the guides and some hunters went to Fire Mountain Camp to hunt. When they got up the next morning and went out to saddle their horses, they found the hobbled horses from Desolation Camp standing peacefully along side of theirs. They had followed them through all the rugged country to Fire Mountain with hobbles on in the dark.

```
     Ted and I are sleeping in one of the wall tents.
We had a sow grizzly and her cubs in camp last
night while we slept. I guess she was after the
caribou meat that was hanging in a tree close to
camp. One of the men in the cabin heard her and
scared her away. Good thing we were so exhausted
after our long ride that we didn't hear a thing or
I would have died of fright after my last episode
with one. We had the head and horns from the cari-
bou lying on the doorstep to our wall tent.
     I rode along with Ted and his hunter yesterday
for something to do. We spooked up an enormous bull
moose but couldn't get a good shot at it as we were
almost on top of it when he spooked and took off
into the bushes. He was sure a majestic sight with
his head held high and his antlers glistening in
the sunlight as he trotted off into the thick
brush.
     Some of the places we go on the horses you
wouldn't think possible. At times I wonder just
what I'm doing sitting on the side of a mountain,
```

freezing and half scared to death. I haven't come up with an answer yet. I keep asking myself the question, are we having fun yet? It's mighty cold up here right now as this camps at about forty five hundred feet. We're still taking lots of pictures and can't wait to see them all.

We had two or three more hunters to take out after this and then closed up the camp for the season and headed back to Fire Mountain Camp to close it up for the season also. Our next stop was Line Lake Camp. After closing it for the season we packed up the entire pack string of horses and headed off down the trail back towards Atlin still many miles away.

Chapter 26

Home

It was late fall now and we had been in the mountains since early June. We were more than ready to come out once again. It was time to catch up on all the news and to spend some time with our friends. We were looking forward to things like a hot bath or talking on the telephone. As we rode towards town the thing that was foremost on both of our minds was a hamburger and a coke. This turned into our main topic of conversation during the last twenty or so miles of our trip. The closer we got to town, the faster the horses walked as they too knew the long season of hard work was over and the time to rest was about to begin.

We would spend the winter relaxing and catching up with everything that didn't get done while we were away. Spring would arrive soon enough and the whole process would begin once again. Living the lifestyle we had chosen to live for these years is certainly not for everyone, but those who do choose to live this way, come to know themselves and the people around them well. They learn that the small things, things as simple as a piece of string or an elastic band can make life so much more enjoyable. Ted and I know we are privileged to have been able to live in the wilderness of Canada's far north and to have seen and experienced nature in all of her moods and shared in all of her beauty.

We have covered many miles of these mountains on foot, horses and snowmobiles and have had the opportunity to see and do things many people only read about in books. We have developed a respect for nature in all of her different moods. We are grateful to have been able to share these special moments with each other and with all of the animals that we've encountered and both feel that our years in the North have enriched our lives tremendously.

Our years spent together in the wilderness have shown us both just how awesome our God really is.

How time and time again when we needed Him most He was always there for us, never once letting us down.

We thank Him for giving us this time together to experience his love.

MEMORIES

MEMORIES ARE SUCH PRECIOUS THINGS
THEY FLY BY US LIKE BIRDS WITH WINGS
AND HOVER DEEP WITHIN OUR MINDS
ERUPTING EACH AT DIFFERENT TIMES
THEY SPEAK TO US OF TIMES GONE BY
THE GOOD TIMES AND THE BAD
OF LAUGHS AND TEARS
THROUGHOUT THE YEARS
EACH ONE OF US HAVE HAD
EACH ONE OF US HAVE MEMORIES
THINGS WE WISH COULD LAST
TIMES THAT MADE OUR LIVES COMPLETE
THOUGHTS OUT OF OUR PAST

Bonnie Traplin

Printed in the United States
24303LVS00005B/178-201